You is for University

Edited by S.L Hyde

Design by Lamplight Press

You is for University: The A-Z Student Guide oon How to Survive

Second print publication in United Kingdom in 2014 by The Student Wordsmith in collaboration with Lamplight Press.

Print by W&G Baird LTD

www.wgbaird.com

Disclaimer

This book details the writers' own personal experiences of and opinions surrounding study at university and the 'university experience'. As such, the author and publisher are providing this book and its contents on a "case-dependent" basis and make no representations or warranties of any kind with respect to this book or its contents.

Neither the author or publisher, nor any contributors, or other representatives will be liable for damages arising out of or in connection with the use of this book. This is a comprehensive limitation of liability that applies to all damages of any kind, including (without limitation) compensatory; direct, indirect or consequential damages; loss of data, income or profit; loss of or damage to property and claims of third parties.

You understand that this book is not intended as a substitute for consultation with a licensed medical, educational, legal or accounting professional, but provides content related to educational, medical, and psychological topics. As such, use of this book implies your acceptance of this disclaimer.

Acknowledgements

Welcome to our second edition anthology from The Student Wordsmith. It is my first volume as both creative behind the organisation and editor of its collections. I would like to thank Loughborough University for allowing me this opportunity. In particular, my thanks must go to its Enterprise and Commercialisation Studio, with whom I have worked for the past fifteen months on developing this product.

Megan Powell-Vreeswijk has been a credit to her colleagues as a mentor throughout this process. To staff in the Marketing departments at both Loughborough University and Loughborough Students' Union, thank you for spreading the word of The Student Wordsmith. To Fran, Jo and Chris (*A Dozen Eggs*), your eye for detail in the creation of our branding was flawless and, to my fellow Studio cohort (2011-14), your continued interest and support during long days in the office has made every one brighter.

This particular publication would not have been possible without the commitment and support of our 2013 competition judges panel: Antonia Bell (*Writing East Midlands*), Michael Jacobsen (*The Business of Creativity*), Jon Osborne (*RadioHead*), Kate Rhodes (*Crossbones Yard*), and Catherine Rogers (*Creative Leicestershire*). My thanks, again extended, to our proofreading and editorial assistants: Rupali Gosai, Beth Hartshorne, Becky Marsters, Chloe Mustafa,

Jonnie Nash and Louise Singleton, all of whom proved incredibly valuable during the editing stages of this work. To our illustrator, Bhavika Sankada, and our typographers Antonia Caranza and Gemma Lazenby, whose expertise in book design I could not have done without, and to blog-owner, Charlotte Huckle, for making the inclusion of recipes in this edition possible through a partnership with her award-nominated, *Lottie's Little Kitchen*.

Last but not least, I would like to thank Lamplight Press for their interest in *You is for University* and their dedication to its final design and production phases. To Loughborough University's English and Drama department, in particular Dr. Kerry Featherstone, for constantly encouraging my passion for creative writing and poetry. I would like to thank our emerging student writers for their wonderfully original works and for their trust in The Student Wordsmith to showcase them.

Finally, I would like to thank my family. To my sister, Rachel Hyde, for her on-going assistance in ideas of design and creativity, and to Georgina Bryan; the mother who taught me from a very young age that if you put your heart in it, anything is possible.

May our university journeys inspire you to create your own.

Sophie-Louise Hyde (The Student Wordsmith; BA., MA., current PhD)

About the Author

Sophie-Louise Hyde is an emerging poet and writer based in the Midlands. With an English degree and Masters in Creative Writing under her belt, Sophie launched The Student Wordsmith as an online platform for students and graduates wishing to enter careers in the writing world.

Alongside this, Sophie is currently working on a part-creative PhD thesis that explores the techniques of verbatim in poetry through an examination of the riots in England during 2011. Her research aim is to create an original range of works in poetry that will engage new audiences and give a voice to those who have previously been under-represented on the subject. As a result, Sophie has been one of five to receive a Glendonbrook Fellowship Award for her research.

Her other interests include contemporary, radical landscape and experimental forms of poetry, collaboration across art forms, and digital literature.

For media and all other enquiries, you can contact her at: sophie@thestudentwordsmith.com.

Contents

A

B

C

VIII

X

Lottie's Little Kitchen

Final Thoughts

Afterwords

Accommodation, n.

HELPFUL HINT:
If you are experiencing problems in your halls or accommodation, there are plenty of people that you can talk to dependent on your institution:

**Hall and accommodation teams,
Security at your university or hall,
Landlords and estate agents if you are living off-campus.**

In Accommodation, n.

Seagulls and sirens merge with one another;
I hear their ululating mating calls
wailing across the city for each other
as I sit, lonesome. And as darkness falls,
the heavy-goods train rumbles through my dreams
with coal-black cargoes of interpretation,
and nothing is as simple as it seems -
spiralling ever outwards to frustration.
The iron-gate beneath my window clangs
open and shut all night, and it grows,
until I cease to hear or feel the pangs.
The people passing and the pleasures tearing,
scheming to wring the dark of all its joys,
in screams and shrieks and roars and endless noise.

'Night in Halls'

Thomas Tyrell

York University

The Arts, n.

Bristles -

stroke canvas frantically
with a force of expression.

An array of fierce reds, and oranges,
as fire burns to stain the vision.

This life bleeds splendid colour.

The brush -
it works so hard
with a mind
FULL –
its oil hitting her heels as she strives for perfection.

Anger enraged, paint burns a hole in the canvas -

It bursts.

Splashing,
Flicking,
Mixing,
Dashing,
for confusion masks the aching pain –

and now, I stand here inhaling its intoxicating
fumes.

I spot a hint of happiness,
in sunglow yellows and skyline blues.

They are holding hands, holding them out to one another,
entwined in hope,
as duty binds their fingers together in a pine-green
land of (what appears to be) –
eternity.
And then, her phone rings;

'MESS'.
Her boyfriend calling about this weekend's visit.

A painting miscellaneous,
A written feeling on a wall,
A meaning interpreted.

She hangs up.
This 'mess' is an emotion EXPOSED.

It is a message LOUD and C L E A R
of human life flashing before my eyes
as an artwork is formed.

'MESS'

Sophie-Louise Hyde

Loughborough University

Accommodation Then and Now, n.

I heard on the grapevine that the New College Hall, closed down in 2007, is now being transformed into a luxurious conference centre and that Latimer House, once scheduled for demolition, has been reprieved. I had left Leicester University College five years before the impressive new Hall opened so only knew Latimer as an annexe of the old single sex College Hall that stood on the main campus in University Road.

The Korean War was at its height, while reminders of WW2 were still all around us in England when I started my undergraduate course at the University College of Leicester in 1951. Bomb sites had not yet been built over, we retained ration books for food and clothing, and there were shortages of everything else including fuel. As I crossed Victoria Park to reach the college's back gate I was not surprised to find it still divided into Dig for Victory allotments.

In that era all fresher females, except for the local women who lived with their parents, were obliged to take up residence in College Hall which consisted of a Victorian stone building attached to a double-storey row of student bedrooms, erected as temporary accommodation for nurses who worked in the Fielding Johnson building during WW1. The Computer Science Centre has replaced that dormitory building.

My 6x8' bedroom was on the ground floor with a tall window overlooking a bleak asphalt rectangle covered in bike stands. There were gaps in the exterior single brick wall on either side of an 18" wide radiator that remained cold until the end of November to conserve our country's fuel. Newspaper stuffed into the gaps kept out the chilly autumn winds that swirled among the bikes, but it proved an insufficient barrier against the rats that frequented the drains outside the tiny kitchenettes where we brewed evening cocoa. Rats were only occasional visitors, but mice were with us every night.

The 'food' rule was easy to keep. We had surrendered our ration books on arrival. I remember we never went hungry. We had substantial portions of potatoes and fresh veg. Tinned spaghetti or cauliflower cheese complemented the meals five times a week. On Fridays we had fish poached in water, served with beetroot and Smash, but on Sundays we enjoyed a roast beef midday meal.

Tapioca and semolina were dessert staples but we were often lucky enough to have spotted dick or even syrup pudding served with powdered milk custard. Strangely, despite the preponderance of starch, suet and dripping, few of us suffered from the weight problems that beset us in later years when we could choose from a vast variety of foods.

Despite the general lack of physical comforts, however, I wouldn't have swapped places with a modern undergraduate. There were less than 1000 students in Leicester U.C. in 1951 and everyone knew nearly everyone; students of all disciplines mixed in the Crush Hall, the Refectory, and at the Saturday night hop. There were rarely more than eight students to any tutorial group, often far fewer. The old padded cells in the libraries made secluded study areas surrounded by a glorious miscellany of donated volumes which had nothing whatsoever to do with anyone's syllabus.

Best of all, however, graduates were in short supply. We could confidently look forward to a job when we left college.

'University Then and Now'

Margaret Penfold

Leicester University Graduate

ereavement, n.

HELPFUL HINT:
If you lose a loved one during your time at university, there are always people to turn to.

Identify your University's Counselling Service or you can try accessing an external charity organisation, for example:

www.cruse.org.uk

Bereavement, n.

The whirring and beeping of this place has become far too familiar. Overly friendly faces in scrubs appear around every corner, beaming, as though oblivious to the crushed souls littered on the floor. 'How are you feeling now Mary?' said slightly too loud, and from a heart that knew there was nothing now to be done. Trivial news is shared around the bed: 'Grandma I got a first overall in my first semester!' and 'you would not believe what the dog did the other day ...' Everyone aware but no one acknowledging the ever-looming future. 'Do you fancy some wine Grandma?', and with that grin it's like she's good as new, cheekily nodding, even though she's refused to drink water all day. Careful not to touch the edges of the glass - alcohol hand gel applied twenty times a day is a nasty shock to taste - a small glass of chilled white wine is poured and passed over. The news starts again, only this time it's stories of Grandad, only seven months taken from us. It's easier to live in the past when you've been denied your future. With the occasional giggle, she listens to the stories, rarely speaking, but smiling contently.

Again with the hand gel, the lift, the awkward passing of other people whose situation is not unlike your own. Only this time she's different: a weak smile, but agitated. 'I just want to go home. I don't want to be here.' Hearts are breaking each and every time, knowing what she wants and being unable to provide it. 'The provisions are being made, we will get you home as soon as we can…', seems like such a pathetic response. All of my life she was strong, a force to be reckoned with; the sight of her pleading to go home is haunting. Amelia in the bed opposite, and 99 years old, is trying to escape again. She is ushered back to bed, Grandma tutting at her. A glimpse of the lady we used to know. Overpriced crisps and mud water for lunch; shifts are given to go down to the café. No one can settle. At home, you feel useless, here, you feel helpless. It never leaves you, when the phone rings, you dread the voice at the end, bringing the inevitable heart-break.

'Numb'

Naomi Bone

Loughborough University

Campus, n.

HELPFUL HINT:
Don't forget to check out if your university offers a campus shuttle service for you to get to lectures with no worries.

A bus timetable and taxi numbers stored in your phone will save time – you never know when that alarm clock might fail to go off!

Campus, n.

old bronze, etymology, south-centre, a list of musty objects, scents, all these come to mind when I look and I think (in parenthesis) about the place, its meaning and I picture – I picture – I picture a tower (and write as one), orienting my views and grasps of a myriad of flavours to a point, key, certain, focused, focused, focused (and settle) – now recall this construct, history, that shoots and swooshes off the hills, around the mound, over the barrow, the dense fog and bracken. The tower still stands; I'll lay me down – in its wake – I'll lay me down, I'll lay it all down; yes, the first foundations, not much, not plentiful but a sure, solid beginning. wooded things, malevolent sprites, things, ruins, buttresses, the first foundations, everything that, if you take a stroll, you go, see, put on your windy-walkie- talkie-face and breathe deep the air

'First Foundations'

Samuel Hardy

Loughborough University Graduate

Campus versus City, n.

To take three stones
   up, is to take three stepping stones again, is to take
   a R I G H T,

                         IMMEDIATELY

                    to the downward drip

                       of the man-made

                 rain that beats heavy

                         and fast,

                         like a heart

                     as it falls upon

             it's cold metal structure.

To take three bricks down,
is to touch three broken bricks at hand,
before a brisk L E F T
where mother nature waits,

               a face,

                patiently,

                  of bristled bark,

              to embrace you in
              its   L   O   N   G   arms,
              and tell you the world is
              okay.

To take three stones
  up, is to touch three bricks d
                    o

                    w

                    n,
                    and sweetly smell
              the scent of melancholy
       of a world that is lost to man.

                         'Lost to Man'
                    Sophie-Louise Hyde
                Loughborough University

City, n.

The lashing rain and skies all grey,
tourists wishing for brighter days.

Walkers run, and runners smile:
they know it'll only last a while.

For this is London and rain's expected,
a cautious forecast, much respected.

A dash for cover, a moment's peace,
a clap of thunder, the clouds release.

But we stand content despite the weather,
under cover, wrapped up together.

We look around and all agree,
there's nowhere we would rather be.

'London in the Rain'

Barton Matthews

Loughborough University

istance, n.

HELPFUL HINT:
Keep in touch with family and friends whenever possible. A phone call can go a long way...

Technology wiz? Why not attempt to FaceTime them or even download Skype to see their smiling faces instead?

On Long Distance, n.

And as we talked for an hour or so eyes chased but never met, but crossed over oceans and onto screens. We tried to swim to others' hearts but glances slipped and drowned in gloss blue void. Our talk was done but lacking that closeness quiet ethereal, borne from one breath and echoed back as rolling tongue unfolded vowels to bear them across the minute gulf and tingle perfect pallid ears. Speech-sated mouths did hunger for more.

And so we said goodbye.

Half-hearted hands raised to embrace, lips poised to dance upon your face, as webcams gazed impassively. Blue, red lights relayed confusedly, these gestures as true feeling. Post-speech a shadow lingered - there would be more, another time, when I'd see true eyes and you, mine.

Was it the Fifties that they said we'd all have robot butlers? Better yet - an invasion of metal, and malice to cling to each other in the unwavering tide, to be sucked down our flesh all burned and ray guns atomise all our hopes, but not this as I sit - all plugged in to a blinking box of twinkling tunes. Your honest face is all cut up, delivered here in pixels, fragments, staccato words - Call quality, connection speed? What could be done to enhance your experience? This muted android's asked.

We'll have to leave unsatisfied, though we have much more to tell. We click farewell, and I arise, still tangled in dark plastic leads.

We had talked for an hour or so and my toes were numb from sitting down. I wandered to a world where gusting winds cross stitched the sky and battered tears fell from bloodshot eyes.

I guess this will have to do, until I next see you.

'On Long-Distance Love (Skype v.6.1.0.129)'

Tom Nurick

Edinburgh University

The Drinking Culture, v.

Four feet, nine inches, the
sign stood above me at five -
need this height to ride.

12-rated, watching
the others watch, miserably,
some forbidden screen.

Friends beep, beep past you, as
Mum still drives you. August
Baby. Still sat, waiting.

Cheers to that. "Drink up
ma boy." "Still on the Pepsi."
Kill time with empty

bottles, break, "down it
in one Fresher", can't stop now -
this is what it's all about.

You're old enough now.
Drink 'til your head is hanging
over the toilet, and

if you're not puking,
you didn't have a good night.
Hold that hair with pride.

Dance the night away
with the other rowdy teens,
numbered all the same.

It's all just brainless
games. Shrug again, laugh it off,
inhale a strong cough

of leftover smoke.
It's all a joke until your
chest begins to hurt,

and your head and eyes
and body parts start aching,
and you realise

that you're growing old.
Too much for you, Doctor says,
as you watch your friends,

miserably. Watch
as the R-rated life slips
slowly out of reach.

Your small son, stood,
waiting to ride. And you smile:

"Don't rush, son. Don't rush."

'Requirement'

Emily Fedorowycz

The University of East Anglia

Education, n.

HELPFUL HINT:
If you have worries or questions about your course, your tutors
are there to guide you!

Check in with them every so often even if it's just to reassure you
that you are on the right track with your coursework.

Education, n.

-isms and -ologies, canons
and classics,
culture police and
literary fanatics.
I struggle to breathe
as I try
to achieve,
unsure as to where
the conveyer belt
leads.

'The Education Factory'

Joe Abercrombie

Brighton University

riendship, n.

HELPFUL HINT:
On your first day, why not keep your bedroom door open and introduce yourself to as many of your flatmates as possible? It's a great way to get to know people and instantly make friends!

Friendship, n.

A student room strewn with cushions and crocheted blankets, the bed frame empty, its mattress pulled to the floor. Textbooks and essay drafts are piled in a far corner where they can do no harm. A tiny TV rests atop an Xbox in the corner. Nearby is a bowl containing a few unpopped corn kernels, some open Disney DVD cases, and a couple of game controllers. These are the remnants of the previous night's nostalgia.

The photographs tacked to the walls seem to be coming unstuck, many of them hanging on by only one determined corner. Three faces reappear again and again in different combinations. A boy and two girls dressed in Hogwarts robes holding wands. The three of them in pyjamas, drinking champagne, wearing party hats. The two girls sleeping in train seats. The same photograph again, but with the addition of drinking straws in the sleeping girls' hair. The three of them dressed for prom with their three dates, people who have since been left behind like out-of-date phone numbers.

The grey light of the English morning sneaks in through the gap in the curtains and tickles the faces of the three sleeping figures on the floor. Their eyes stay closed. Thoughts of adulthood and the outside world have been spirited away to make way for dreams and they aren't yet ready to wake up. Sleep has softened their faces. Despite the boy's beard and the girls' leftover makeup, they look like children. The brown-haired girl's hand moves, blindly searching for a spare corner of a blanket to cover her exposed shoulder. The boy, who slept in the middle, readjusts his blanket so it will cover her too. She finds his hand and squeezes it as a silent thank you, a gesture that soon descends into a sleepy game of thumb wrestling. She wins. He encircles her waist with his arm and snuggles closer to her, nuzzling her shoulder with his cheek. She opens her eyes and quickly closes them, deciding that the darkness is better. He is still holding her hand.

The red-haired girl rolls over, so all three of them face the same direction. She presses her face into the boy's back, blocking out the light that attempts to invade her eyelids. Her socked feet, patterned with Pokémon, peek out from under the layers of blankets.

The boy smiles and the brown-haired girl feels it. The breathing of the three friends falls into sync as they fall in and out of sleep.

Somewhere from within the folds of the makeshift bed, music begins to play.

"Powerful booty, finding the booty

Give me the booty, wake up booty

Breakfast booty, lunch booty

Supper booty, dinner booty…"

The alarm continues to sing. The red-haired girl groans as she sits up and begins to peel off blanket after blanket. She finds the phone, silences it, and flops back down. She covers her face with her hands.

"Sorry you guys." Her hands muffle her voice.

"Mhmmm."

"I have to leave for my lecture soon."

The red-haired girl makes no indication that she ever intends to move. There is a swish from the hall as a large envelope slides through the slit under the front door and stops by their feet. All three open their eyes and frown at it. The boy tilts his head slightly towards the red-haired girl.

"Grab it for me", he says.

"Why do I have to get it?"

"Because you're the closest and I can't get it because her head's on my arm."

The red-haired girl sighs, sits up, and crawls towards the door.

"Sorry. Am I killing your arm? I'll move", the brown-haired girl says.

"No, it's okay. You have a very light head."

"That better not be a way of saying I'm stupid."

"You're grumpy in the morning."

The boy pulls his hand out of her hand so he can tickle her. Her body tightens into a ball.

"Stop! Stop it!"

He stops.

"I'm not grumpy! I'm lovely in the morning." She tosses her hair dramatically, whipping him in the face with the ends.

The red-haired girl tosses the the parcel over. There is no address, just the boy's name.

"Who's it from?" the brown-haired girl asks.

"I dunno."

He tears it open at the top and turns it upside down, pouring the contents onto his chest: condoms, in a variety of brands and flavours, with brightly coloured wrappers like lollipops that have lost their sticks. After a moment of silence comes the laughter, the boy's the loudest of all. He picks up a Post-It note that has fluttered out with the contraceptives. He reads it, laughs even harder, and then crumples it into a ball and throws it into a corner of the room.

'As the Light Sneaks In'

Sarah Bouzanis,

University of East Anglia

Grief, n.

HELPFUL HINT:
If you find yourself needing to deal with grief, check out your
university's student support networks and/or centres.

Volunteers run some of these centres; they are there to listen
and support you through the more difficult times.

Dealing with Grief, v.

Don't perch me upon a cotton cloud
Or quarter me by the country lake;
No fields of grain inspire me now,
Nor misty hues above the creek.

I have seen too many daffodils,
And belle bluebells, too, pall my soul;
These mocking-jays do not arouse
A drop of woe, a drip of joy.

Instead set me off upon a barge
Where the shadows meet, by day or night;
Off to a shade where silence unites
With her soundless charms of quietude.

And leave my haunt with little tint,
A monochrome wind, a fickle farewell,
And write to me once every fortnight
From the confines of your recent grave.

And here let there be no robin's song,
No blackbird's lay, no warbler's hymn;
Leave me be in my rusty cage:
The throne of human creation.

'Rusty Cage'

Arka Basu

Loughborough University

Graduation, v. and n.

She left her Blackberry for an
i-Phone 4S today, and
I just missed my bus.

Stupid graduation, and growing up and stuff.

Two minutes feel like an hour when the
bus is late -
And you're ill… again.
I HATE LIFE.

Stupid graduation, and growing up and stuff.

No feeling of relief when you get your coursework
- DONE. Instead,

'I've Googled fit celebrities for an hour'.
Stupid graduation, and growing up and stuff.

Now Bud is a lonely beer,
poor Bud.
Stupid graduation, and growing up and stuff.

'Upon Graduating'

Sophie-Louise Hyde

Loughborough University

Saying Goodbyes, v.

Goodbye to the butterflies that crippled my stomach,
every time I spotted your face
half a mile away,

down Paxton Street
where we'd meet, to hide
beneath
endless pillow-dreams, and sheets;
a nest made only for two.

Goodbye to the evenings of dining for two.
Although we both knew that I couldn't cook,
you'd still always
let me try, with
a sweet smile,
and a lie;
"Thank you, that was really nice."

Goodbye to enduring Premiership football on my
telly
and to the fact that I quite liked
your slight sculpt of a belly -
the result of endless beers with the lads at the bar.

Goodbye to boy talk,
and to tickles in the dark,
to the bacon sarnies that
sizzled -
almost as hot as our late-night love making,
and goodbye to the treacle sponge.

And goodbye to splitting that tub of Choc Fudge
B&J's

with a bent tablespoon,
before spending the night, bent -
imitating that spoon,
as I slept among the ruins of hope that the moment
would never end.

'Goodbye to Ice Cream'

Sophie-Louise Hyde

Loughborough University

33

ealth, n.

HELPFUL HINT:
Make sure you register with your local medical centre and GP as
soon as possible.

This may seem trivial but could save you vital time when trying
to access those cures for that headache!

Health, n.

It'll all end in tears. That was the fear
That I was singing in the beginning
But who knew I would be winning
And yet still wet from all these tears
I'm blown away, I've blown my mind
And I've grown in so many ways
It's 'cause I seized the day, you say
I say, a little luck jumped on the train
I bear in mind the times I cried
And sobbed half-dead upon your bed
Not walking away, you hold me instead
'I'm stable!' I lie, you make me able
Of all the gifts the Gods could bring
Of all the ways they could let me in
Through the rings of fire and mental stings
The year is up I wouldn't change a
Goddamn thing

I danced with romance but fell for the mess
As unholy stress overwhelmed the rest
But I remain blessed, it's true, you see
I've learned to love life and learned to love me
I scream 'no regrets' and it feels the best
Shit may just happen but watch us move on
We're gone, like a shot, we're chasing those lots
We'll never regret a night we have lost
Remember forever, decisions I make,
The people I play, the hearts I may break,
My own broken soul stuck up with Sellotape
That's borrowed from friends 'til needed again

But I love it, I love the pain, I love
Days where we do something insane amongst
Volcanic urgency and the mundane

And you know what
Goddamn it!
I would do it again

Living in London, falling in Love
Loving this life like nobody does
Ruined plans, one night stands
Panic attacks are the norm with us
Smokey skies, teary eyes
Forgotten nights
when we smashed the town
And there's always time for
One more
Beautiful
Breakdown.

'Breakdown'

Aaron Parr

Queen Mary University, London

*I*nternationalism, n.

HELPFUL HINT:
Keep your eyes peeled for any societies that you might like to join.

These can provide peer-to-peer support for individuals – helping to keep homesickness at bay.

International, adj.

何谓教育？教书育人，非授之书而习其句读者也。

"教"是知识层面上的丰富、拓展，而"育"来自于对精神领域的关注、培养。但凡一个完全人格的建立，需二者相辅相成，缺一不可。当一个社会高速发展的同时，知识的更新速度也日渐提升，如今我们再难以寻找到当初那种无欲无求、寒窗苦读的求学精神，更多的人开始渐渐流于表面，急功近利地追逐一些所谓的终极梦想。这实在是辜负了当初的大学精神，也违背了教育的本质。

大学教育，作为未成年人到成年人的过渡地带，作为学校与社会之间的平台，应当肩负起二者所赋予的共同使命，如果说学校为一个人成长的前十八年奠下了成长的根基，大学便是穿插于二者之间的一个跳板，大学的上方是社会，人们从中小学一路走来，蓄十余年之力，在大学的跳板上演习数遍，最终一跃而起，跳到社会平台的某个领域里。

社会平台其实也并非仅仅一层，在社会之中还有无数层小平台，平台的高度决定了你成就的高低。也许你从大学之中一跃而上某一高领域，也未见得会再创新高。在大学你学习的是跳跃，是积攒自己的力量，而到达社会领域不会再有一块新土地供你驰骋跳跃，这时候大学的作用就显而易见了。在大学之间你积蓄力量，力量从一定程度上决定了你跳跃的高低，但大学终究是一个人拓展自己的最佳实践地，很多人一生学习到的最宝贵的东西或许莫过于高中和大学的知识。因此，大学应当在个体成长中起到承上启下的作用，在跳板上你无所顾忌得跳跃也不至于跌落下来，而跳跃的同时你收获的是生活的经验，把握到的是自我的能力；大学教育也应当是严谨却又宽容的，宽容你的一次次错误，允许你在各个领域对自己的潜能进行挖掘，而走出大学，你带走的不仅是广博的知识储备，更有宝贵的生活能力，你的意志，你的信心，你的勇气，你的思考，等等这些，构成了一个真正完美的个体，而你仍需再度经受社会的考验，一步步深加工，最终走向成功。大学给予你创造奇迹的可能，你充满信心的未来从此开始。

再回到大学教育本身，大学给予个体的是独立思考的能力，正所谓"心之官则思，思则得之，不思则不得也。"而在这思考

'Whatever that golden moment may be, cherish it, inform yourself and make your choices sensibly.'

When a student enters the realms of higher education, it does not just serve to house their thinking but enlightens the student, allowing them to freely explore their potential. To teach someone is to enrich their way of thinking through the means of learning and acquiring knowledge. However, to educate someone is to do more. Education sheds light on the capabilities of an individual and broadens their horizons. As a result, that person becomes more independent in thought, will standout further from the crowd and fosters his own individuality. He becomes better-rounded and is more prepared for his entry into the world of industry.

As society continues to accelerate at full speed, the growing pace in the wide-variety of knowledge that is available within academia can lead one to panic; the student becomes eager to strengthen his own abilities and is desperate for the instant benefits in doing so. He will read and talk critically but this may no longer be in sheer delight of the material. Instead, his focus sits firmly on that modular exam that he must pass or, indeed, that deadline which he must make. One strives for success but at what expense?

There is no doubt that the world of education offers the student a chance to contribute to the world in which we live, gaining valuable qualifications in their chosen area of study and in the extra-curricular

的基础之上，允许有不同思维的碰撞。大学使每一个个体都拥有了充分表达自我的权利，表达自我不是为了张扬个性，而是为了在相互对答之间更好地体会知识，体会生活，体会我们所处的世界。

苏格拉底式的问答式哲学思辨模式在今天仍有很大的用途，通过问答引领探求者不断思索，不断揣摩，最终达到真理，正所谓迷途者问路，教育所给予的不是一个完整的路线图，而是通过一块块小标志牌指引你去追寻属于自己的目的地，答案并不唯一，真理也只是探求内心所得到的对生活的恍悟，当你最终抵达目的地，回首一路走来的路，你会充满欣慰，因为那不是一条盲目追寻而得出的路，而是你自己凭判断凭知识思索探求出来的路，路线清晰地浮现在你心底，此时你收获的不仅是真理，还有一步一步走来培养出的独立人格和坚韧品质。

大学教育就是这样一个平台，它应当不指引，点到即止，任由学者自品。倘若每一个求知之人都能够如此，在求知的道路上秉持着自己的判断、依循着自己的理性去思考去决策，并充分地表达自我，交流内心，那么每一个个体所获得的精神世界都会是多元化的，人人都可以成为彼此的老师，在观点与观点的对峙之间，真理慢慢地浮现。通往真理的大道有无数条，而凭自我的思考和努力探索出来的唯有一条，在大学里，独立思考不仅仅是一种能力，更应是一种习惯。

大学教育，究其根本，无非是为了让更多从大学里走出的人能够为未来奠定下一个坚实的基础，由此我们就需要改变传统的教与学，而是形成一种双向式的思辨模式，教者也可从师于学者，学者亦需受引于教者，人人相互学习，社会便形成了一种昂扬向上的学风，不仅个人能够因此进步，社会也会在此力量的推动下将知识推广到一个新的深度。W

在此浅析大学教育，简拙之言，在此祈愿教育的润泽能够如同细水长流，浸润每一寸孜孜求学者的心，愿更多的人在此寻得方向，不再迷惘。

愿与诸君共勉。

activities offered. In this sense, university is the pond that houses the tadpole and, as the student waves a fond farewell to his childhood, he takes his first swim out into wider waters. The student embarks upon a journey of self-discovery; one of growing responsibility, personal development and sheer determination and hard work. Moreover university is the springboard to a credible career and most who have been lucky enough to experience it would claim it was the best time of their life. For the most part, I would be inclined to agree.

However, that is not to say that university is the be all and end all of one's life. There is a great significance placed on seizing the day and cherishing your moment but how much of that is done from behind your laptop screen or sat at your desk during endless hours of study? Some students would suggest that this is where they cherished their moment most. Others might be motivated to propose otherwise. Your moment, for example, might be in bagging your ideal job straight out of school or even in travelling the world. It might be buried deep within the deferred gratification that comes with a university education. Either way, whatever that golden moment may be, cherish it, inform yourself and make those choices sensibly to ensure you can make the most out of your moment.

'The River of Education'

Wanyue Yang,

Edinburgh University

obs, n.

HELPFUL HINT:
For advice on how to go about securing your ideal job, being well-equipped for interview, or even producing that cracking CV, visit your university's Careers and Employability centre.

You may have to book an appointment in advance if you require a longer chat with them.

How to Land the Perfect Job, n.

Post-university life can be stressful, but to ease you in, here are a few top tips on writing a good CV. Although it might be the last thing on your mind, your CV is something you really should be thinking about while at University...

1) Lay it out. Think about the order in which you present your CV. What is your most impressive section, your education or your work experience? TOP TIP: Make your CV as easy as possible to read and make sure everything is in date order (with your most recent dates at the top).

2) Stand out from the crowd! Take part in extra-curricular activities while at university. As more and more people are getting a degree, it can be the extra-curricular activities that you do outside of your course that make your CV stand out.

3) Short and sweet. It is likely that a potential employer will not have much time to read through a lot of CVs. Make sure you keep yours to a maximum of two pages long. TOP TIP: Bullet points are a god send, they prevent long winded sentences and make the CV look tidy.

4) Secret admirers. Don't give specific referees at the bottom of your CV. Simply write the phrase, 'referees available on request'. This not only saves you some room, but also allows you to choose the most appropriate referees for each job.

5) Don't be repetitive or repetitive or repetitive.... If you've already mentioned "admin experience" in two previous jobs descriptions, do you need to mention it in your third? Or could you instead think of other things about that job that you could mention that adds something new to your CV?

6) Sorry! Wrong number! This might sound like an obvious one, but do make sure that all your personal details are included and kept up to date.

7) Sell yourself. Don't make your Personal Profile too self-involved. It's great that you enjoy swimming and hiking, but what is it about swimming and hiking that makes you the right person for the job? What does your potential employer want to hear? TOP TIP: A good way to avoid this is to make sure that you use words such as 'competent' and 'adaptable'.

8) Simple but stylish. It might sound obvious, but make sure that the text is in an appropriate font and size that an employer can read! Also make sure that style and format is consistent throughout the CV. TOP TIP: Use size 10/12 for content and 12/14 for headers and only use bold or italics in headers.

9) Time traveller? Try and avoid gaps in time in your CV, or at least have something in mind that you can say in interviews and applications to explain gaps in employment or education. Doing charity work is a good way to fill gaps between employment and show a potential employer that you are willing and keen to work. TOP TIP: If you have lots of little gaps, this can be hidden by using just years in your CV. E.g. 2009 – 2010.

10) Most importantly, don't lie! You will get found out.

Erm... Great, I have a CV. Now what do I do with it?'

11) Dress to impress. Think about what your CV is selling, it's selling you. So if giving them out to employers in person make sure you look the part. If you say in your CV that you are smart and professional, look smart and professional. If you say you are a good time keeper, don't turn up to hand your CV in five minutes before the business closes!

12) Always follow up. If you haven't heard anything from a place that you've handed your CV to after a week, either give them a call or go in and see them. Let them know that you have applied for the position and are wondering if they have short listed for interview. TOP TIP: Remember to start the conversation with, 'Hi, my name is…'. There's no point showing you're keen if they don't know who you are!

'CV Top Tips'

Louise Singleton

Loughborough University Graduate

HELPFUL HINT:
Learning and developing knowledge can be about more than just those really high grades.

Don't fall into the trap of comparing yourself with your mate who always gets First Class marks. University is as much about personal development as it is about obtaining that degree!

nowledge, n.

It's a Knockout, v. and adj.

You only live once, and you've gotta make it count.

When living is
the food in the fridge wearing thin,
Basics pasta, and endless tins of baked beans, but
plenty of empty booze bottles in the bin,
is it all really worth it?

Three intellectual consonants, BSc, and
cash going out quicker than it goes in.

Where's the priority?

Whoever said that we
have it easy
should walk a mile
in my size four shoes –
and then tell me that I'm crazy.

Because waiting for that next hit
of your student loan
is like waiting to go
twelve rounds with Mike Tyson, and knowing –
It's a Knockout.

But it's okay, anyway,
because education is a valued commodity? '

'It's a Knockout'

Sophie-Louise Hyde

Loughborough University

HELPFUL HINT:
One of the biggest worries for most students is how to balance and budget their finances.

Whilst your student loan might seem like a great amount of money, you will have plenty of expenditure to bear in mind when budgeting.

Keep an Excel record of your income and expenses, and why not talk to student support for some extra help on how best to keep hold of your cash?

Loans, n.

Experiencing Love, n. and v.

It's Friday Night, and I'm
checking my Facebook regularly,
to identify a fading personality
that I once knew.

'Sorry, it's too soon to add this person
back to your Block List';
I guess I must have forgotten this,
sat staring into my mug of tea, as
pictures of your mug last Friday night
are taking over my newsfeed.

'Who am I kidding?'

I could go back and follow you again on Twitter,
but I'm not some crazed, lovesick bunny boiler, and
I'm pretty sure it won't let me in
on the secrets of your new relationships -
not like Facebook can.

So I'll just trawl through your past statuses...

There's still nothing, and
'nothing is still what I feel' I lie,
as the girls call me up, and
I fight the urge to give in and cry.
'What kind of idiot am I?'

I mean, I know
I can't cook and
I burnt spaghetti that one time I tried, but
you're the only one who gets me
with that silly look in your bright blue eyes

I still get butterflies just looking at
your pictures.

I counted: 1,975,
and I'm LoveBlind -

It's Friday Night, and I'm
checking my Facebook regularly,
to identify that fading personality
that I once knew.

'LoveBlind'

Sophie-Louise Hyde

Loughborough University

*M*entality, n.

HELPFUL HINT:
Worried about a friend or not quite feeling yourself?

Help and advice on mental health issues is available from your
Mental Health Support Team.

A problem shared is a problem halved.

Your Mental Health, n.

Now you can have it all,
C A R E L E S S   F R E E D O M.
Those cheap bottles of that
Sainsbury's finest plonk,
8% white that you never fail to devour.
Those Screwdrivers and Nasties
that he bought you
never were quite to my taste.
As your six-inchers stick to the floor,
I never could stick the noise of Rihanna
pounding through the room.
Please Don't Stop The Music...
A scramble for the keyhole in

the black of night with
Papa Si's chicken nuggets and chips.
The aroma seemed to smell so good to you,
but I could never stomach it.
Rows and rows of your very own library
in paperback:
Austen, Hardy, Woolf,
and your favourite –
Emily Bronte's Wuthering Heights,
'a tale of star-crossed lovers'
sit watching with me
as you waste your hours stalking Facebook addictively.
Pictures of last Friday.

That day I opened that
heavy wooden double door
to a world with no room for 'madness'.

A   -   V   A   S   T   -   and empty
space
filled with nothing but fear
and a station for water
that could make anyone need the toilet.
Never mind the anxiety.
'I'll need you to just fill out these forms provided
please, Miss'.

You could have heard a pin
drop
in the silence
had it not been for Dr. Rahinda's and Dom's conversation
or the constant calling of the phone.
But you don't know, do you?
That you can't ever get rid
of that sense of shame that buries itself in your
clothes
down to the tips of your socks -
'Anxiety and Depression', the pamphlet on the side
read –
as I sat waiting for what felt like days,
e n d l e s s -

Some call it an illness, but
I know you'd call it 'diseased', 'unstable',
and in the time it takes you
to take d
       o
        w
         n,

in liquid, that absinthe,
my name is on the dotted line,
and I can't erase what is happening to my brain
as I sink into the chair, feeling sick at the sight of it:
'Counselling Service'.

It's just another L .I .F .E. to you though, isn't it?
One invisible, shaming, unknown disease,
And it's mine.

'L.I.F.E'

Sophie-Louise Hyde

Loughborough University

Musicality, n. and adj.

I place my hands on middle C,
to try my hand at Debussy.

For despite my unacquainted ear,
and motives that remain unclear,

I really want to learn this piece
to let the modern day decease

and float along in days gone by,
where I never have to say goodbye.

For here I sit to play those notes
that once a minstrel would have spoke

"Hear the finest work in all of France
and do not dare to miss the chance!"

So concert halls fill to capacity,
with patrons of such strong voracity;

for all whom the music captured
sat silent, still, and lay enraptured.

For his great work transcends the ages
and year on year it fills the stages;

for magic lies in those black notes
that so long ago he wrote.

His presence in this world so missed,
Debussy, the great impressionist.

'Ode to Debussy'

Barton Matthews

Loughborough University

Mentality, n. and adj.

Why did I come here? That's a stupid question. I came here for the same reason everyone comes to Oxford: to get a good degree, to get a good job, to get rich, to get happy: simple steps.

The steps… you'd never imagine from outside how ugly they are, a bright yellow band running across each one, denying the inside of the bridge any integrity. You couldn't miss them unless you stared at the roof.

If I'm here for the same reason as everyone else, why do I feel so separated from them all? I was expecting toffs from Harrow and Eton, but they're not all like that. That stereotype is unfair. It's just that everyone else here is "passionate" about their subject. So am I if you look at my personal statement, but I think deep down I've always known that they were empty words.

Don't get me wrong, no one forced me into this. For the past few years it has been me alone who has been saying that I wanted to study English Literature. It was only because of this that my mum and teachers have encouraged and helped me to do the best that I could, so that I could go to the "best" possible university. I bullied my subconscious into submission. As usual, I've only myself to blame.

I reach the top of the steps.

Why have I allowed it to get to this? Eight weeks into a degree I hate, feeling like my life is essentially over. Yes, I like reading, but don't most people? That doesn't mean they should do an English degree. I'd sooner pick up a copy of *Heat magazine* than anything by Dickens. That can't be a good sign.

I was in the English Faculty Library yesterday, surrounded by people poring over literally dozens of books at a time, and all I could think was "why?" Who cares what Blake or Chaucer meant? They were just single men (not women, notice) in history who had opinions and could write consistently. But we live in 2013; surely we should be writing new stories for the simple purpose of entertainment? If you want politics, flick Question Time on. If you want sixteenth-century politics, then yes, treat yourself and wipe the dust off your Shakespeare collection… but why would you?

And don't get me started on poetry. What sick bastard invented the poem? And why did it catch on? If I said today that I had a great idea for a new TV show where no one says what they mean (the temptation to revert back to Question Time is tenacious) and there are long, vague scenes in which people and places all represent something else entirely, I'd be picking the colour-padding for my cell before I could say "to be or not to be" (the most ludicrously overused and overrated quotation I've ever had the misfortune to study). It wouldn't work on TV, and it doesn't work on paper either.

I remember expressing to Mr Jenkins, my A Level English teacher, this bewilderment over our obsession with poems and old literature:

"You want to be an author, right Beth?" was his initial response.

"Well, it's a possible career option, bu–"

"So yes. Have you ever heard, then, of the expression 'standing on the shoulders of giants'?"

"It's one of Oasis's weaker albums," is not what I said. I'd heard him use this cliché before, so I had come prepared:

"Yes sir, but do you not think it's possible that if we spend so long admiring the giants' shoulder blades, we could become too obsessed and never climb higher?"

'Bridge of Sighs'

Simon James

Lancaster University

Mental Wealth, n.

University can be great fun, but being away from home for the first time, whilst trying to manage study, work and life commitments can be pretty tough. Whether you've experienced difficulties or not, everyone has 'mental health' and we all need to take care of our minds. StudentMinds' 'Top 10 Tips for Maintaining Mental Health' can help you along this student journey.

1) Get Involved!
There is so much going on at university so why not make the most of it? University is about developing yourself as a person, not just an academic, so visit your Students' Union to find out how you can get involved with clubs and societies.

2) Do Good to Feel Good

Helping others by deliberate activity has a positive impact on our own mental health. Visit your Volunteering Centre to discover opportunities on campus, in the community or in the great outdoors. You'll meet new friends whilst learning new skills, making you all the more attractive to future employers!

3) Start talking about Mental Health
Talking to others about your feelings can seem scary, but are not alone. Everyone is NOT always having an amazing time. Like you, they struggle sometimes. Like you, they feel better when they talk about it. Talk to people you can trust about how you are feeling; your parents, friends, tutor. If you're worried about a friend, start a conversation - your understanding could be just what they need.

4) Don't be afraid to seek help

If you broke your arm, you'd seek help. It should be the same principle for your mental health. 1 in 4 of us will experience a mental health problem or disorder, where we may need help from a specialist. It's important to get help when we need it to prevent difficulties becoming more serious. Problems with money, housing, relationships and studying are all common causes of worry, but universities have support services that exist to help you. And don't forget to register with your GP!

5) Find study techniques that work for you

Everyone has a different study style so play around to see what works best for you. Revising in bite-size chunks and then taking a 10 minute break can help with memory retention. If you find it hard to motivate yourself, see the study support on your university's website - at least you will be using your p rocrastination for good!

6) Have a Healthy Body for a Healthy Mind

Eating sensibly and getting the nutrients we need has a good effect on our mood; a bit of exercise will release those good endorphins. Just a regular walk round the park can make a real difference!

7) Take time to Relax

Many students will juggle multiple responsibilities whilst at university, so it's crucial that you build in time to chill out. Why not try something new, like a

Yoga class or meditation?

8) Don't forget to sleep

A lack of sleep not only causes tiredness but has also been associated with mental health problems. If you live in a student area, a proper night's sleep can seem impossible, but getting the recommended 7 - 9 hours will leave you best prepared for the days ahead.

9) Remember 'You don't have to go out'

There are certain social expectations when we go to university, but remember you don't have to do anything you don't want to do. People that you would want to be friends with will respect your decisions, so do what makes **YOU** happy.

10) Go Offline

Research has shown that spending too much time on social media can have a negative effect on our mental health, so try to cut down where possible. If you love the internet, do something useful like visiting sites that can help with your mental wellbeing, they will help you make the best of your student life.

StudentMinds' top tips have developed out of our national network of mental wealth groups, ran by hundreds of students across the UK, campaigning to help all students make the most out of their university experience and beyond.

Top 10 Tips for Maintaining Mental Wealth'

Rosie Tressler

StudentMinds

HELPFUL HINT:
A busy nightlife and student parties are a big part of the 'university experience'.

However, always remember safety in numbers to ensure that you and your friends are well looked after on journeys to and from your local bars and clubs.

ightlife, n.

I lay there in the darkness. Listened to no one, looked at nothing, alone. The bed was half empty so I half expected that I'd fall straight to sleep, but my insomnia danced around his absence. It was exhausting.

I tried to put this time to use. Earlier in the day, I'd have given anything for a few moment's peace, some time to nurture my own thoughts. This is what I should be using these sleepless nights for I told myself; now I have plenty of time, I should be putting it to use, clearing my head, rearranging my thoughts so I can handle tomorrow. But I couldn't. It was the depths of the darkness that wouldn't let me concentrate. Even when I shut my eyes, there it was, looming over me, pressing itself into me; a reflection of my sorry-self, lying on that half-empty bed. Tired and weak. Scared.

62

I closed my eyes, used every ounce of energy to tense every last part of my body, took a deep breath and started to plan the day ahead. Get up, straighten nightdress, open curtains, make bed, wash face, clean teeth, brush hair, dress, downstairs, boil water, light fire, make breakfast, make breakfast stretch to seven, make sure there is enough for dinner, make sure dinner can stretch to seven, wake Jack, smile, be nice, be lovely, wake children, wash children, David's arm, Frances' temperature, find Church clothes, dress children, check Denzil's hem doesn't need to be taken down, give children breakfast, take Jack breakfast, ask about his day, see that children have finished breakfast, make sure clothes are presentable, tie shoes, wipe faces, fix hair, find lipstick, find good handbag, find cleanest hanky, find hat, find hat pin, cover up dirty hair, ask Jack if he is coming to mass, gather children, deep breath.

And that's what I did. In that order… more or less. I wrote a note and stuck it on my muddled heart so I wouldn't forget that today, I had decided to be happy.

'Notes on a Love Story'

Aisling Lewis

Loughborough University

Originality, n.

HELPFUL HINT:
If, like the writers in this collection, you love to write or would like the chance to try it out, check out the university, local and online groups available to you:

www.greatwriting.co.uk
www.writers-online.co.uk
www.thestudentwordsmith.com

For Originality, adj.

I am the ways to worry.
You are the cave-man art that throws a flood of light.

I am wishing that I had freedom.
You are wishing for the richness and variety of these
works of art.

I am thinking about the washing up.
You are thinking they were conceived as splendid
and powerful creatures.

I am suggesting that we need to pick up milk.
You think the challenge must not be too severe.

I am thinking about the organisation of my life.
You say the beginning of civilisation was retarded.

I am tired from too much madness.
You regard it exclusive possession of a secret
spiritual knowledge -
revealed directly by God.

You are the cave-man art that throws a flood of light.
I am still thinking about the washing up.

'Cave-Woman'

Sophie-Louise Hyde

Loughborough University

ick, n.

HELPFUL HINT:
With the numerous sports and extra activities to choose from whilst attending university, take your pick of your favourite hobby and enjoy!

Bear in mind that some societies will require an annual joining fee and account for this when balancing your finances.

Editor's Pick, v.

"So there I was, sitting in the field, and this cat just comes up to me and sits on my knee. It just stared up at me with its big eyes, and I knew."

"Knew?"

"Knew it was proof that aliens do exist."

I am not sure what I had expected as an introductory conversation from one of my fellow Masters students, but this was certainly not it. The bespectacled boy looked at me with a smile. His words poured out with a Midwestern American accent that made me think of fireflies and the prairie and hot summer winds. I was also fearful, because finding a sane, liberal-minded person from my homeland would be akin to finding a cricket pitch (no, Kansans, not the black, chirping kind).

"Right," clipped the instructor with a bemused crook of his eyebrow, "shall we get started, then?"

The class took place around a table, four students and a lecturer flipping open crisp new notebooks bought especially for the start of term. I suppressed the urge to write the title of the course in bubble letters across the front cardstock page. I am mature. I am a Masters student. This is serious.

***

Our foursome spent the day at the ruins on our own as the lecturer called a mechanic. It suited our creativity to be left to our own devices, anyway. The Chinese student was in raptures over the ducks waddling along the pond's edge, and the Brit and the American began to bicker (a beloved pastime they shared). I walked alongside them, staring at the low castle wall and shielding my nose from the cold.

"Maybe I'll just write a poem if I don't have time to do a story," he said.

"Excuse me?" She replied.

"Ya know, just come up with some poems. It'd be easier."

"Babes, poetry is not easier than writing stories."

"I dunno. The word count wouldn't be as bad."

"Really? Really?"

And so they went, the American egging on the Brit, just as he had done from day one. I feel that, deep down, they both revelled in the banter. This was supported by their general friendship and the scarf that the American knitted for the Brit over Christmas break. They reminded me of an old, smugly married couple who had grown so used to one another that they no longer censored themselves.

***

"A 67?" I typed furiously into the e-mail I was sending to my lecturer. "I put a lot of time and effort into my work, and I just thought I would have earned a better grade than that. I'm so disappointed." I had failed to convert my score from the UK scale to the US scale.

And so, with my dissertation outline in hand, I have thought back on my experience abroad, and of my first foray into the postgraduate world of academia. The lessons I have learned will stay with me throughout my writing career, and can be applied to my everyday life as well. Earthworms can fall in love with flowers, adlets are offspring of misunderstood and often prejudiced marriages, poetry is harder to write than prose (but if I think it is not, I can always knit a scarf as a peace offering), and, if all else fails, I can use my frustration to scare a lecturer to the point of assumed decapitation.

'Organis(z)ed Chaos of an American Postgraduate'

Amanda Bigler

Loughborough University

Quintessence, n.

HELPFUL HINT:
There are many 'quintessential' or stereotypical views of the university student. However, by no means are these correct opinions...

University is as much to do with personal growth as it is anything else and, for that reason, you are in charge of your journey.

Just take control and be yourself!

The Quintessential Student, adj.

So the sun arrived and here I stand,
overjoyed and somewhat tanned.

The shorts were out, the shades were on,
the last vestige of winter gone.

A day spent lying on the grass,
as I watched the world go past.

Peering over many pages,
a story read throughout the ages.

So take a moment to sit and smile;
I'm sure it will only stay a while.

'Summer Term'

Barton Matthews

Loughborough University

Recipes, n.

HELPFUL HINT:
Don't panic if you have never cooked for yourself before; 3 years
is plenty of time to master it...

Local supermarkets often have recipe cards for you to grab on
your weekly shop and the Internet is a great source for learning.
Plus, let's not forget our very own student recipe section at the
back of this book for you to get started! (See Page 119)

Relationships, n.

Her eyes open, the birds are singing, the day has taken over, and everything looks still. The walls have edges and all the things in the room make it look messy. And his eyes are open. She realises she is still cuddling him in an amorous way. He glances at her, and she glances back; they both look away. She tries to disentangle from his embrace but he just moves his arm so that they are still with each other in a different position. His arm is under her neck and she is lying parallel next to him.

"Would you like to talk?" she asks him. She is not whispering because she knows he finds it weird when she does. But her voice sounds too rough for the morning; it feels like it is hammering on the walls. He scratches his chin.

"Sorry?"

"Should we have a conversation?"

"Uh, what?"

"I was only suggesting. We don't have to; I can go."

"Heck, it's 5:30 a.m."

"Oh," she answers; she never gets the time right based on the singing of the birds.

"What would you want to talk about?" he says smiling slightly. She considers asking him about his favourite colour.

"Did you sleep alright?"

He laughs, "Yeah, yeah, I slept okay."

She nods; she feigns a smile. The room is so silent; why is he awake? His snores usually fill the gaps in between the noise. And everything seems to glimmer in an obscurely familiar way, the massive weights on the floor reminding her that she is in bed with an incredibly fit guy.

"Um, a friend walked in on us last night," he tells her.

"What do you mean?"

"Like, he walked in while we were asleep."

She narrows her eyes, "Johnny?" she asks.

He laughs, "Yeah."

"That's awkward."

"He found it funny," he rubs his eye, "maybe he even appreciated it." The awkward joke he isn't supposed to make.

She looks around: white and more white, but the covers are blue. Ocean blue, she remembers describing them on her very first night here. "So what course do you do?"

"Politics", he answers.

"Mm, I thought so."

He narrows his eyebrows.

"Well I thought it was something like Geography or History or a Social Science."

"Why?"

"I saw you at that debate."

"Hun, you've been following me?" The second awkward joke you don't make to the girl who's been Facebook stalking you for the past two weeks.

"No," she smiles.

He hasn't noticed her embarrassment. The ball is in his court to make conversation, but he's looking at the cracks in the ceiling and she's getting bored.

"My ex also came from Argentina." The one thing a boy does not want to hear when he wakes up naked next to a girl.

"Was he suave like me?" he asks instead of rolling his eyes.

"I don't know, are you suave?"

"Um, yes."

She smiles, "I suppose so then."

He pulls the covers up; perhaps he thinks she's too naked. The lights are still off, but hints of the sun are seeping through the curtains and she can see the tiny hairs on her own arm stick out in white. She's hungry; she's always hungry. He closes his eyes. She looks up at him and she knows what's happening; he's done this before.

'The Sense of a Beginning'

Naomi Poltier

University of Exeter

Remembrance, n.

Remember when we went camping
and brought shining fire to the bush?
A reminder of all the luck you danced on.

One night in August, swaying
on the yellowing hilltop
that overlooked our hometown.

Amulets and saints, guiding me
across the thinning grass.

Between each tiny fragment,
teenage rituals carried out at dusk,
hanging with meaning.

The changing signs of freedom
lurking deep in the treasure chest
underwhelm our eager hands -
melted plastic of a previous gathering.

Between each tiny fragment
we were the watchful eyes,
dug out from boxed piles
promising to keep them safe.

The cuornuciello clings
to the chain around my neck.
Amulets and saints, guiding me.

'Bonfire Hill'

Chiara Di Paolo

Loughborough University

HELPFUL HINT:
Remember the health risks that can come with adulthood and be sure to familiarise yourself with both your University Medical Centre and local Health Clinics or Hospital...

Play it safe!

ex, n.

78

An Encounter with Sex, n.

<u>The Boys</u>

'What type of learner are you?'
said the checked tie
with the pit stain.

Kinaesthetic: e.g. Liam Connery.

The do-er.
Enjoys physical challenges.
Xbox controllers stacked muscles
on fingers
for bra strap flicks
and pushing knickers
to one side.
Is more likely to locate
the G-spot accurately
than the ...

Auditory: e.g. Jonny Atkinson.

Never presses mute.
Ears finely tuned to squeals and
switches in breathing patterns.
Will often spot if she's faking
leading to high marks in self-doubt

unlike the ...

Spatial: e.g. Jason Crawford.

> Learns best with visual aids.
>
> Two nipples and painted nails
>
> onscreen,
>
> traded for ringtones
>
> and chips at lunch.
>
> 'Course I won't babe, for my eyes only'.
>
> They all thank .coms for
>
> their best moves
>
> and their best afternoons.
>
> There was one category missing
>
> and no one thought to pay attention to the note-taking
>
> minute scribbler in the corner
>
> whose rebellion was a Star Wars t-shirt
>
> under his school shirt
>
> e.g. Adam Fraser.

> Never afraid to tell his mother he loves her,
>
> unless Liam Connery, Jonny Atkinson or Jason Crawford,
>
> hands cupping their crotches like basketballs,

are nearby. Their word for

that bit in between girls' legs terrifies him

only slightly less than the thought that

his mother must have one.

He justifies his lack of popularity amongst his peers

with the thought that he'll scrap the puppy fat one day.

It's likely that

at the school reunion

2020

they'll all be there:

Liam Connery: Personal trainer. Divorced.

Jonny Atkinson: Telesales. Type two diabetes.

Jason Crawford: Unemployed. Down to six a day.

And they'll notice that

Adam Fraser

hasn't done too badly for himself.

The Girls

The uniform revolves more around
Jane Norman bags on left shoulders
than knee length skirts
and single gold studs
glinting from ears
that already knew more
than their parents did
at their age.

They wrote their own
whoever 'they' were
a dirty merge
of Bobbi Brown Tampax
and slaps on arses
echoed in giggles.

They wrote their own
on toilet walls
smeared in mothers' lipsticks
scrubbed from handbags
wrapped in codes:
Joe Russell is fukin haaaawt!

Chernice = BITCH!

and, perhaps, the most hurtful of all:

Alicia will alwayz be a vergin!

Those eyeliner smudges controlled us
more than any
drawing pin on a noticeboard
ever could.

The obsession of the school bell
timed fake orgasms
on car seats
burger boxes
and last week's maths
stuck on hot backs

The boys were measured in inches
The girls in inches down their throats
and neither minded sharing.

Exit interview:
them: have you lost it?
me: yeah
them: blood?
me: a drop or two
them:
congratulations ... B+

Please fill in the blanks using black pen only

He ___ the start of a sentence.

He ___ the one who looked good with a tan.

He ___ the 'lovely lad' according to my mum.

He ___ the revision distraction.

He ___ drank water through a headache

and laughed at my crackled and burst Paracetamol packets.

He ___ the one who cupped my chin to the Cribs,

and didn't let go until the Courteeners,

too young for Not Nineteen Forever.

He ___ the one who was truly happy that weekend in Putney

when we were roped in a duvet

blinded by an un-blinded window.

He ___ the one who wasn't the one after all.

He ___ the one who made me feel stupid

when he showed those photos

to those lads

I ___ the one who let him.

He ___ the one who made me feel small on New Year's Eve

because it was easier than

He ___ the one who could still call when things cracked.

'Attitudes towards Sex Education'

Natalie Moores

Loughborough University Graduate

Your Sexuality, n.

It isn't difficult at all, in theory or practice. There are people in the world who have to walk barefoot for miles in the baking heat just to bring water to their families, bleed their fingers under sewing machines for insulting wages, sit through four hours of chemo in a bleak hospital - people who have actual, soul-and-stamina-breaking hardships to deal with.

All I have to do is tap ten or twenty words onto a screen and touch 'Enter'. That is literally it. So why is it one of the most breath-suspending things I find myself ever having to do?

Maybe it's the fact that I only had the revelation ten minutes ago, and am too overwhelmed as a result, too bombarded by transmitters and nerve impulses as my brain tries to make sense of this.

I never, in all my teenage years, imagined being in this situation: a swift tidal wave of change, submerging me alone in my desk chair, at the end of Freshers' Week. I expected challenges of a more domestic nature: overflowing washing machines, getting to a lecture 59 minutes late. I did not expect a "Defining Moment of Character" revelation.

I'm not totally self-absorbed: this is obviously not the most dramatic thing that's happened to anyone in the history of everything, in the new millennium, or in my generation. But on the infinitesimal thread of my lifespan, at least, it's a big deal.

If asked, I wouldn't be able to provide a precise date for when I stopped being a child and turned into a young adult. However, at 3:16pm on Friday the 12th of October, in the newly personalised shoebox that is my room, I can tell you exactly when this happened.

I look at my phone, having put in two contacts as the recipients: my closest friends from sixth form back down South, the ones who know my strange personality inside out. What are they going to say? Will they reply instantly? Or will I have to check every five minutes for three agonising hours until they finally get it?

My hand continues twitching; I haven't calmed down one hundred percent. Homeostasis is an ongoing process.

I've been at university for exactly five and a half days. Tomorrow my flatmates and I will dive into the excitement of the Societies Fair, and I know I'll sign up to about twenty different things. Hence my browsing the Student Union site for the umpteenth time, to see if there's anything else that might pique my interest.

Out of languid curiosity, I clicked on the 'Campaigns and Representation' tab, and then the LGBT page - why not? The group at my old sixth form gave some fascinating talks every now and then, and human rights is an avenue I'm keen to explore further. The uni one has a pretty rainbow on its homepage, with more orientations in its spectrum than can be fitted into a concise acronym. That's where I saw the word, familiar but strange at the same time.

'Ace'

Lexy Hudson

York University

Sport, n.

The lecture hall resembles a floating field of lilac. They're everywhere; a plethora of purple hoodies all smiling and chatting about their successes the previous afternoon. A quick scan reveals the subtle differences: university rugby club, university hockey club, rocket ball society, all integrated as one purple mass. The lecturer walks in in her gym kit.

Being involved in a sport team grants one a certain element of status within the campus. Sports teams open up a whole new avenue of social interaction. The friends made in sport can ease one into university life, and often play a vital part in one's university experience. As soon as the sporting fixture reaches its end, the social activities begin, often lasting well into the night.

Sport offers a whole host of new opportunities for individuals, and the nature of sport at university ensures that individuals often get to undertake these opportunities in world class facilities. In my first year I took up a sport that I had never heard of. The sport is not particularly popular, but the infrastructure at university ensured that, after a certain degree of success within my new team, I was given an opportunity with the national side for that sport - something that I never would have dreamed of before university.

This is the beauty of sport at university - you can have a go at anything. In their second year of studying, my housemates, having seen the value of sport at university (and so they could proudly wear the kit around campus), all decided to take up a new sport at university. After umming and arring their way around the fresher fair they opted to try for the mixed lacrosse team. After a few training sessions two decided it wasn't for them, one lasted a season and the other is still playing now, two years later. Despite this, all of them made new friends, had a new experience and were able to feel the pride in representing the university at sport.

As can be seen from this, sporting success is not compulsory; neither is wearing the African purple of the athletic union. Many of the individuals who play sport at university will never win a league, trophy or competition. But that is not important. What is important is that everyone enjoys themselves, meets new people, learns new ideas and tests themselves, processes which are easily aided by the great deal of support given by the various players, staff and environments.

The majority of my memories from university have a sporting foundation; not necessarily through playing, but more through the experiences that sport has given me, through the friends I have made and the opportunities it has provided. Through sport one makes lifelong friends, friends of all shapes, sizes, ages and cultures. Although it is clichéd, one's sporting team truly does become an extension of one's own family. This family shows no greater pride than when there is mutual success, notably in the winning of leagues and cups. Before coming to university I had never won anything. After three fantastic years of enjoyment I leave with three gold medals, one England cap and a whole host of new friends. What could be better?

'Better Than Sport'

Seth Burkett

Loughborough University Graduate

Support, v.

An empty chair centre stage. A Powerpoint presentation is projected, it flicks at speed from slide to slide. Dan stands downstage left. He is in his late teens. He does not sit on the chair.

Dan: Fast, so fast.

> This lecturer can talk fast.
>
> I can't even think of a comparison, but it's really fast.
>
> So, he'll talk fast and I'll write fast - yep, that's the plan.
>
> To be writing.
>
> Fast.
>
> Lecture room,
>
> Everyone's following protocol
>
> They're writing,
>
> And writing fast,
>
> Not even breaking a sweat
>
> But I can't -
>
> I can't write fast.
>
> Can't keep up.
>
> So I don't.

I'm just staring.

Gaping.

My mouth's catching flies.

"It's important", I know, thanks for emphasising that.

"You need to make sure you write all this down".

All of it?

"I can't stress this enough"

Alright, fine.

I'll try mate.

I'll try.

Fast, so fast.

This guy can talk really fast...

The difference between Linear and Amorphous is... erm... what? Amorphous...

Anorphous... Amblorphous... how the hell do you spell that?

Sounds like a digestive problem my cat has.

Ah, I missed it. I knew it! And that was important.

He said it would be important.

Sylvie, what was that? What was that he said?

The difference between Amporborlous and Linear?

I think it was definitely important.

Sylvie?

Sleeping.

Great thanks, Sylvie.

You'll be asking me for a copy of my notes later won't you?

Well, guess what, I haven't got any.

I never have any.

Sucks to be you.

Fast, he's so fast. I just can't keep up. Why bother.

Pen on the table.

"Maybe you should get tested?" my mum always says.

"Go to the disability office," my mum always says.

"You might be dyslexic," my mum always says.

Dyslexic? I'm not dyslexic.

Look to my right,

Stephen sits.

Stephen's clever, Stephen's a worker, he'll have got the note.

The all important notes.

Notes, Stephen, notes. Come on, just let me see.

"Amorphous/ Linear difference important".

That's all.

That's all he's written.

Doesn't even need to write it.

He knows the difference between Amorphorlorous and Linear,

Knows he knows it.

Stephen's clever, Stephen's a worker.

But I'm not stupid…

What was that? A new type? A type of structure?

Wait, I wasn't listening.

Is it on the handout? Nope, not on the handout.

But it was important. Had a high level of importance.

A "this-is-so-important-you-need-to-write-it-down-so-that-you-learn-it-so-I'm-not-even-going-to-put-it-on-the-handout" level of importance.

Balls.

Why bother?

"Just pop into the disability office," my mum always says.

"Don't they just do informal drop in things?" my mum always says

"You don't need to tell you mates," my mum always says

There's nothing wrong with me.

I don't need special treatment.

Fast so fast, it's just that this guy's so fast.

Stephen doesn't think he's fast.

But I'm not Stephen,

But I'm not stupid…

What's that?

Stephen's nudging me.

The difference between Linear and Amorphous?

He's asking.

The lecturer's asking.

He's asking me.

I can't answer.

Notes, are you any help? I didn't think so.

Even if the answer was in there, I couldn't read it.

The three lines that I have were written by a three year old.

Stephen? Help?

He mimes something.

I don't know what he mimes.

"It melts?"

There's a snicker in the room.

It's not my fault. He talks too fast.

I'm not stupid, I swear I'm not,

I'm just…

I don't know.

He talks too fast.

Dan exits. The chair remains empty.

'He Talks Too Fast'

Louise Singleton

Loughbororugh University

ime, n.

HELPFUL HINT:
Never underestimate how quickly your time at university can go.

Plan wisely; keep a diary of coursework deadlines and an eye on those jobs opportunities to ensure you don't miss out!

~~How~~ Time ~~Flies~~, n.

Well I know babe, you've made it loud and clear,
The time we spent together I'll always hold dear.
But while I've still got you, and while you're still
mine,
Perhaps we could at least pretend, just one more
time.

I know it's over, the end for you and me,
That's what you want, and I've had to agree.
Tomorrow I'll be alone with my cigarettes and wine,
But before that darling, just for tonight, just one
more time.

I'll be okay babe. You said yourself, it's not me, it's
you.
Go out and be free, do what you've got to do,
You know what I'm like. I'll always be fine.
But please, just for now, just one more time.

So don't worry about me honey, don't let me hold
you back,
And if on some day you think of me, I'll be thinking
of you right back,
But till then baby, I still want you by my side,
Just one last request from me, just one more time.

I'll remember what you said to me, you said that
life's a test,
And you'll do better now you're not settling for
second best.
So I hope you find that one, and I hope they treat
you right,
But right now I'm here, so maybe just one more
time.

And though you're leaving, I'll be there in
everything you do,
You might be over me baby, but I'll never be over
you,
So while you're still mine, help me make it through
the night.
You said it'd be forever, but now I'll take just one
more time.

'Just One More Time'

Jonnie Nash

Loughborough University Graduate

HELPFUL HINT:
It can be hard for some students to settle in at University, following the move from home comforts to a brand-new environment. However, there are plenty of people for you to talk to if you begin to feel homesick.

Look out for your University's student-led support groups. These networks are there to offer a friendly ear and helpful solutions that might help you beat the blues!

University, n.

University, n.

He started off small.

He was a bright idea, thrusting himself out of the ground with a force powerful enough to drive up buildings around him. Soon they were full and their inhabitants bustling, creating knowledge like steam. Under the life-giving nectar he grew, his boundaries stretched against themselves. The delicate hum of machines, the scratch of pens; they were like tonic energising him to do more and be more. But he had to be patient and wait his turn. He had to learn to enjoy the work, and wait. Until, one day, they handed him his title. Which he accepted with a modest smile and triumphant tears in his eyes.

A University.

He was not as old as his brother or sisters, nor was he as wise and as appreciated, but he was there and he was proud. Life became about achievements and advancement. He wanted his halls to glitter gold, silver and bronze. How many awards was it possible to fit into one place? It was limitless, and so was he. Potential was his middle name and he would be damned before he would stop trying to squeeze every ounce of greatness from his people. Stopping, after all, was not in his nature.

He was progression wrapped up in a welcoming smile and an open book. But in the beginning he had been small and he had to work to be recognised on the world stage. He had dressed cleanly and smartly in front of his siblings. It was only right to keep such a clean slate and nice appearance when he had such idols to contend with, but he was more than ready to strip off his peacock feathers and get down with the boys.

Because, of course, at the start it had been just boys. The lads, the guys, all of them strong and fighting fit, ready to take the world by storm. He taught them all he knew.

They had all scoffed when the women flocked to the doors, demanding education and rights, like they were entitled to any of that. But he was young and small, and he liked to think of himself as modern. Screw it, he had thought, take them in. Let these ladies show him what they'd got.

And, by god, they did.

The new year saw new faces and new names. Different tongues fought battles in every corner of himself and he learnt them all. The world was no longer a small space and people travelled for hundreds of miles to be taught in his home. He was small but the world was large. It was foolish to sit and wait for the world to catch him; he had to go out and get it himself. Sometimes he laughed at his brothers and sisters for their prudish ways, marvelling instead at his own sense of expansion.

He was everywhere at once. At parties he was the nice guy no one had invited but everyone knew; a colourful character that could drink like the best of them but still be sober enough to lead people back into his awaiting gates. In the exam-hall he often chose to sit at the back and pit his own knowledge on his own exams. It would never do to be lazy, and what example would he be setting for his students? Every essay, every test, he was there. At every sports match he screamed and cried with the rest of them, painting his own colours with pride over his cheeks and glowing with the sense of family.

He grew to dislike the word 'student' for its lack of intimacy. These people were more: they were his children. He had no favourites because they were all his favourites. The quiet ones and the loud ones, the little and the large, boys and girls, black and white. There were no distinctions inside his doors, no labels. He took them all.

He watched each and every one of them grow and develop. When they entered his gates, rattling boxes full of excitement and new beginnings, they were young. Small, delicate creatures he adored and cherished for their fresh insights and open hearts. He moulded them and polished them and sent them on their way with feathers in their caps and pride in their hearts. He was always happy to welcome his children back for more. The more the merrier after all.

He thrived on the learning and the masses of people that entered his gates and halls. Sometimes, he thought too long and hard on the passing years, but he was always reminded of the people that made him. Even the ones that moved across the world, onto bigger and greater things, were still a part of him. He was at the centre of every social web, links like golden chains spanned out from his centre, and he could feel them all in his heart beating away at their hall chants and mantras. He smiled to think of the lives he had changed and how, in turn, they had changed him.

'Of Small Things'

Natalie Jackson

Loughborough University

irtual Networks, n.

HELPFUL HINT:
The Internet is a wealthy source to anyone studying at university.

It's vast range of information on any number of topics means
that it can provide you with the material that you might need
for an assignment.

However, always check with your department that the website,
book or article you are referencing is of academic quality if you
are unsure.

~~Honouring~~ Virginity, n. and adj.

"- And the poppies blow
Between the crosses, row on row."

Pushing up the petite daisies,
his movement becomes the suicide
of her once purest moments.

They lay in the midst of desolation.

Her tender tombstones the
ample headstones of painless pleasure
as he is gone to a better place
across the sea of lily-white sheets.

Entwined,
what is his camouflages with hers
and he soldiers on in his mission
to combat her mortal heart.

"- And the poppies blow
Between the crosses, row on row."

The tragedy that is his tongue
takes itself
six
feet
under
in the time of their darkness.

Thunder roars inside her,
as the horror of what his hands are doing
stress the signs of an early funeral.

Loved, and now we lie:
'The Burial of a White Chrysanthemum'.

"- And the poppies blow
Between the crosses, row on row."

Red blood oozes beneath her;
red blood and a war, already won,
as the battle lines that mark their place

----

blur her perfect vision.

As her life flashes before her eyes –
she watches charcoal ashes scatter.
Spirit of spirit,
He is the flesh of her flesh.

"And the poppies blow
Between the crosses, row on row."
And his seed not laced in love, but sex,
still leaves her wanting more.

'The Final Act'

Sophie-Louise Hyde

Loughborough University

HELPFUL HINT:
There are many things that you can do to ensure your own wellbeing.

Making time for yourself and your friends, eating well, and regular exercise are just three of the ways that you can keep yourself going through all the hard work!

ellbeing, n.

Looking after your Wellbeing, n.

Overwhelmed, these nights roll into one;
Choked tears fear fast approaching day.
It's all too much; I've come undone.
Sat dialling, trying to focus on
That soundless neon kebab shop hum
And the voice saying,

"It's okay."

'Nightline'

Jenny Carter

Queen Marys University, London

e *X* ams, n.

HELPFUL HINT:
Exam season can be a highly stressful time of the year for any university student but there are plenty of ways to avoid overloading yourself...

Plenty of water, a regular revision routine including breaks, and a pocket of pretty-coloured highlighters are all essential in preparing yourself for those all important papers!

Examinations, n.

Plaid purple runs and
paving stones
move beneath my feet,
as I face
a date with
destiny.

Ten tiny tables
and the tapping of twenty pens,
or the keys of Zoe's laptop,
mapping out what happens next –
the key to Zoe's future.

The leaves of lecture notes
are flut-ter-ring
as the leaves of Loughborough's winds
take flight again.

Zoe takes her place in line, again.
Among the finalists,
among the library desks,
among the
silence –

'Mobile phones are to be switched off,
and please do not consume food or drink'.
Welcome to Level 2.

Plaid purple runs and
paving stones
move beneath my feet,
as I face
a date with
destiny:
to the library.

My final ever set of exams.

'My Final Ever Set of Exams'
Sophie-Louise Hyde
Loughborough University

$\mathcal{Y}$ou, n.

HELPFUL HINT:
Remember: your time at university is about you and what you
love to do.

Never be afraid to just do what you love!

You is for University, n. and pron.

If I were to put ten seasons in a shell—
Seasons by calendar, not by faith,
Though the latter dearly needed—
From ten seasons ago to yesterday,
All to rest in my first term bubble:
Greece breeze from my send-off.
Bursting boxes awaiting boarding.
Tube-lost twenty-first moments.
Fresher's plunge. Festive frivolity;
Honorary sistership, Lovespeak sown.
Basted bird. Firelight Sudoku.
Thumbs up for British justice!
The largest Family—Sunday afternoons,
Clicks of knitted fingers, marbles and dice.
Slow-cooked generosity, richly warming.
Growing passions, rolling new plots
Around the tongue to test,
Expelling the sour ones. A three on paper.
Chester, Exeter, Torbay palms.
Prestatyn Sands and the Liver Birds.
Discoveries. Fonder for home.
City smog giving way to gulls,
Air salt and crystal strawberries.
November words, lined with stardust;
Swirling smoke in a vivid blue.

Painfruits. Penned and in heart.
Honey stings as a reminder.

'Nutshell'

Alex Harlequin

The University of Middlesex

est, n.

HELPFUL HINT:
A zest for life is essential if you want to make your time at university worth it.

Now, go and grab every opportunity that heads your way!

For the Zen Master, adj.

I'm the centre of calm, I am the Zen Master,
Think my thoughts slow, as you think yours faster.

I'm the part of this world, so beautiful and rare,
Where troubles and woes just aren't allowed there.

Serene and at peace, it all becomes clear,
What was holding me back was that whore known
as fear.

Now I've sent that bitch packing, I'm as free as can
be,
This Zen Master knows and he sees what he sees,

Sees through all the shit, sees through all the lies,
Sees through the hard life, sees through 9-5s.

No longer blinded by doubt and despair,
I feast on this new world, I breathe in its air,

As I glide through the days, and take in the nights,
Getting high on the fumes of carefree delights.

The burden of worry, the weight of concern,
I've thrown on the fire, and smile as they burn.

Goodbye to the past, goodbye to before,
Goodbye to the struggles, goodbye to the bores.

This life is my own, this life's down to me,
To choose my own path, to choose being happy.

At one with myself, at one with it all
This peaceful motherfucker is now standing tall,

'Cause Zen is my mind, and Zen is my soul,
Zen is my mantra, which now makes me whole,

Zen is the light, and Zen is the way,
I am the Zen Master, so hear what I say,

These are my words, and my words they are true:
Zen is to be, and to be is to do.

'The Zen Master'

Jonnie Nash

Loughborough University Graduate

Lottie's Little Kitchen
food, travel and life♥

My name is Lottie and I'm the creator of Lottie's Little Kitchen, a food blog dedicated to making student cooking beautiful and delicious. I'm currently in my third year of an English undergraduate degree at Loughborough University. When I'm not writing essays I love to cook (can you tell?), watch films and go walking.

Recipes Included

Beef and Vegetable Pie

Mackerel, Spinach and Pepper Rice

My Grandmother's Vegetable Soup

No yeast pizza

Vegetable curry

Falafel pittas

Student roast chicken

Birthday cake

Chocoholic's brownies

For more recipes check out my blog:
lottieslittlekitchen.blogspot.co.uk

A little kitchen a lot of food!

Beef and Vegetable Pie... (serves 4)

There is something quite special about serving up a beef pie. You can really play with what you put in; Potato, turnip, parsnip – whatever is kicking around in the fridge. This short crust pastry is easy to handle and not nearly as daunting as it seems.

Pie Ingredients

250g diced stewing steak
2 potatoes,
peeled and chopped
4 carrots,
peeled and chopped
6 mushrooms, sliced
1 large onion,
finely chopped
50g plain flour

1 beef oxo cube
1 tbsp marmite
2 tsp mixed dried herbs
Salt, pepper

Pastry Ingredients

400g plain floWur

200g unsalted butter & diced
4 tablespoons cold water
1 egg, beaten, for glazing

Method

1. Heat a pan with a little vegetable oil and cook the potatoes, carrots, mushrooms and onion for 5-10 minutes, until the onion is soft. Whilst the vegetables are softening, in a bowl mix the flour, salt and pepper together. Add in the stewing steak and make sure each piece is coated in flour. Add the floured steak to the pan until brown and sealed.

2. Tip the contents of the pan into a slow cooker or oven proof dish. Then crumble the oxo cube into a mug, add herbs and the marmite and fill the mug to the top with boiling water. Add to your slow cooker and then cook on low for 4-6 hours or at 180°C for 2 hours. I would advise you leave the filling to sit over night, but you can use it straight away.

3. To make the pastry, pinch the flour and butter together in a large bowl until a breadcrumb consistency forms. Then add in the water and work until a ball of pastry forms. Divide into two thirds and one then roll out the larger portion to fit the bottom of your pie dish. Spoon in the filling and then roll out the second piece of pastry. Cover the filling and slice a cross on top of the pie. Brush with an egg and then cook in an oven preheated to 180°C for 45 minutes. Serve with greens and mash if desired.

Mackerel, Spinach and Pepper Rice...
(serves 2-3)

This is one of my favourite meals for a night in with a film. Mackerel is such a tasty fish and is packed with healthy omega three. Double win. This recipe is also great for your exam period as it's packed with brain-boosting ingredients.

Ingredients

6 shallots, finely chopped

100g spinach

2 handfuls frozen peas

300g cooked rice

200g smoked mackerel, flaked

1 red pepper, sliced bunch

coriander leaves, roughly chopped lemon, sliced in 2

Method

1. Heat a little oil in a large pan then add the shallots and peppers in and fry for 5-10 minutes until softened. Meanwhile wilt the spinach by putting in a colander and pouring over boiling water. Refresh under cold water then squeeze liquid until dry.

2. Add the peas, rice, mackerel and prepared spinach to the pan. Season and stir until the peas are defrosted and the dish warmed through.

3. Stir through the coriander leaves and then serve with lemon wedges. Make sure to spritz the juice over before eating.

Spinach and pepper?
All sounds a bit fishy to me.

My Grandmother's Vegetable Soup...
(serves 4)

Caught freshers flu? Got a tonne of essays to write? Can't be bothered to cook anything whatsoever? Never fear, this vegetable soup has got your back. Ridiculously straight forward to make, this soup is just waiting to warm you from the inside out. It's a hug in a bowl.

Ingredients

1 courgette, trimmed and chopped

1 leek, trimmed and chopped

2 large carrots, peeled and chopped

1 can chopped tomatoes

1 vegetable stock cube

Salt and pepper

"What lovely soup you have there Grandma..."

Method

1. Put all the vegetables into a large saucepan and crumble over the stock cube. Cover with water and add in the tomatoes. Simmer for about 20 minutes until the vegetables are soft.

2. Transfer to a blender and whizz up until smooth. Pour back into the saucepan and season to taste. Serve with crusty bread.

No Yeast Pizza... (serves 2)

Put down that dominoes menu! This is one of the easiest and cheapest pizzas that there is. It is now one of my weekly staples and yet always a treat. You can top your pizza with pretty much anything you like, so great creative!

Quick tip: you can get away with 1 ball of mozzarella but if you like your pizza super cheesey, you can use 2

Ingredients

240g plain flour

120ml water

1 tsp salt

1 tsp baking soda

Glug of olive oil

2 tbsp tomato puree

1 tsp dried mixed herbs

1-2 balls mozzarella, sliced

75g pepperoni

1/2 green pepper, sliced

Method

1. Mix the flour, salt and baking powder together in a large bowl. Add in the water and work until a dough forms. Turn out onto a floured surface and knead until the dough is smooth. Roll out to a thin base and transfer to a baking tray.

2. Pour on the olive oil and spread across the base. Mix the tomato puree, herbs and 2 tbsp water together in a mug and then spread across the base too. Put on the mozzarella, pepperoni and green pepper. Put into a oven preheated to 190°C for 15 minutes. Serve with salad and wedges if desired.

No Yeast?
No problem!

Vegetable Curry... (serves 4-6)

Ingredients:

2 sweet potatoes, peeled and chopped

1 small cauliflower, trimmed and chopped

1 can chickpeas, drained

1 red pepper, sliced

1 red onion, finely chopped

1 piece of ginger, peeled and finely grated

1 clove garlic, finely chopped

1 red chilli, deseeded and chopped

3 tbsp curry paste

Bunch of coriander, leaves removed and stalked finely chopped

1 tin chopped tomatoes

1 tin coconut milk

100g spinach

Glug of vegetable oil

Method

1. Heat the vegetable in a large, deep pan. Add in the onion and curry paste. Mix together and cook for 5-10 minutes until the onion is soft.

2. Add in the ginger, chilli, garlic and coriander stalks. Cook for 1 minute and then add in the sweet potato, cauliflower and chickpeas and cook for a further five minutes. Add in the tomatoes and 150ml water then simmer for 30 minutes, or until the sweet potato is cooked through and the sauce is thickened.

3. Stir through the coconut milk and pepper then cook for five minutes. Stir through the spinach before serving. Serve with coriander leaves, natural yoghurt and a little rice.

This curry will freeze happily for up to 3 months once cooled down

Falafel Pittas... (serves 2)

During my time at university, chickpeas have become a big part of my life. Sounds kind of sad, but they are so versatile and always a cheap addition to my shopping trolley. Falafels make a wonderful, speedy meal at any time of the year and you can put them in pittas, wraps, burger buns or simply have them on their own.

Ingredients:

400g chickpeas, drained

1 small red onion, finely chopped

1 garlic clove, finely chopped

1 tsp ground cumin

1 tsp ground coriander

1 tsp chilli powder

2 tbsp plain flour

Handful flatleaf parsley, finely chopped

2 tbsp vegetable oil

4 pitta breads

4 tbsp hummus

2 tomatoes, quartered

2 handfuls green salad

Method

1. Mash the chickpeas, onion, garlic, parsley, cumin, coriander and flour together in a bowl with your fingers or a fork. Shape into 8-10 balls and set to one side.

2. Heat a pan with the oil and fry the falafel balls for about 15 minutes until browned all over. Whilst frying, toast the pittas, split in half and spread with hummus. Line with the salad and tomatoes then add the falafel balls. Serve with extra salad if desired.

Anyone fancy a Pitta Falafel?

Student Roast Chicken... (serves 2)

There is something about a roast dinner that reminds me of home. Being able to recreate that homely feeling in your student kitchen is an important skill to learn. I know the timings can be daunting but this step by step recipe has got your back.

Ingredients

1 small chicken

2 good glugs of olive oil

1/2 lemon, quartered

2 cloves garlic, crushed

1 bay leaf

Drizzle of honey

3 carrots, peeled and sliced

4 small potatoes, peeled

Salt and pepper

Method

1. Stuff the chicken with the garlic, lemon and bay leaf and drizzle in the honey. Then rub the entire chicken with a glug of olive oil and season generously with salt and a little pepper. Roast in an oven preheated to 180c for 1 hour and 30 minutes, or for as long as advised by weight of the bird.

2. With an hour until the chicken needs to come out, parboil your potatoes, drain them, shake them and set aside in a saucepan with the lid on. With 15 minutes of chicken cooking time left, add your second glug of oil to a baking tray and heat in the oven for 5 minutes. Once hot, tumble in your potatoes and carrots. Roast for 30 minutes.

3. Take your chicken out of the oven (your vegetables should have been roasting for 10 minutes) and turn the oven up to 200c. Rest the chicken for 20 minutes until you're ready to serve. Reserve juices if you want to make gravy. Serve the chicken with roasted vegetables and extra greens if desired.

You cooking dinner?
Or are you chicken?

Birthday Cake...

As much as your friends might appreciate shots of tequila for their birthday, their livers, heads and 4,000 word essays won't thank you for it the next day. I much prefer to give my super-easy but pretty fantastic student birthday cake. And at the end of the day, who doesn't want to eat cake on their birthday?

Ingredients

225g self-raising flour
225g caster sugar
225g butter, softened
2 tsp baking powder
4 eggs
4 tbsp strawberry jam
For the icing:

150g icing sugar
2 tbsp butter
1 tbsp magarine
Splash of milk
1 tsp vanilla extract
Sprinkle, to decorate

Method

1. Break the eggs into a large bowl and add in the sugar, flour, baking powder and butter. Mix together with an electric hand mixer until well combined. Divide evenly into two greased and lined sandwich tins and bake for 25 minutes in an oven preheated to 180°C. Do not open the oven door before the cooking times up or the cakes might cave in.

2. Leave the cakes to cool in the tins and then turn out. Cover one in the jam and then place the other cake layer on top. Then combine the icing sugar, butter, margarine, milk and vanilla extract in a bowl until a smooth icing forms. Spread the icing all over the cake and then sprinkle on as many sprinkles as your heart desires.

There's always a need for cake, especially on Birthdays!

Chocoholic's Brownies...(makes 12)

I have not yet met a person who refuses a brownie. If you're that person, you need to try this recipe. I challenge you to refuse another ever again. They are that good. Moist, a little gooey and decadently rich.

There's a lot of addictive things around...
Chocolate's denitely the best!

Ingredients

275g plain chocolate, broken into pieces

100g white chocolate, broken into pieces

275g unsalted butter

325g caster sugar

175g plain flour

1 tsp baking powder

4 eggs, beaten

1 tsp vanilla essence

Method

1. Melt the plain chocolate and butter in a heatproof dish over a pan of simmering water. Once completely melted remove from the heat and stir in the sugar. Add the eggs and vanilla essence

2. In a separate bowl sieve the flour and baking powder. Then fold this into the chocolate mixture along with the white chocolate.

3. Pour the mixture into a standard brownie lined with baking parchment and bake in an oven preheated to 180°C for 25 -35 minutes (depending on how you like the consistency). Allow to cool completely then slice into squares and serve.

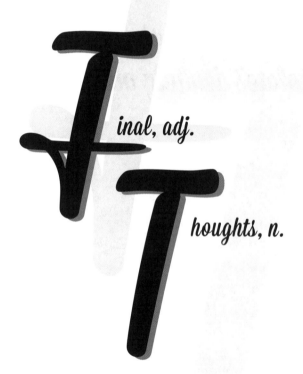

Thoughts, n.

'...And don't forget that toilet brush.'

Yes, you heard me correctly – perhaps not the first thing you'd think to pack, but picture this: Its 8:50AM after another wild night out. Your lecture starts in ten minutes. You can make it. Forget breakfast, all you need is to get dressed, destroy the alcohol breath (toothpaste: another must) and most importantly, empty your bladder. But wait. What is THAT in your toilet? Here I'll let you fill in the blanks – You're regretting not packing that brush now aren't you?

Ok, so you've just finished your lecture (I'm assuming you're wearing clothes, so I won't include them on this list) and your belly is starting to rumble since you deprived yourself of pizza for tea last night in favour of another vodka shot. This leads to essential items number two and three: pasta and sauce. Food for the Gods. Whether it's dinner or tea (don't try to protest about breakfast being missed out: do you really think you're usually going to be awake before midday?) pasta equals perfection. Near impossible to burn, ready in fifteen minutes and deeply satisfying, it's still cheap enough for you to be able to afford another night on the tiles.

Now you've come back from a 9AM, had a nap, eaten your pasta, taken a shower since you haven't yet washed since yesterday (shower gel, shampoo, towels, check them off right now) and you're dressed in the same, slightly soiled clothes from last night because you don't want to do any laundry. But wait! Where are your keys? You can't leave the house without them. This is where you need THE POT. Your pot may be that mug you didn't want for Christmas, or the free plastic pint glass from fresher's fair. Always keep your keys in the pot. It's as simple as that. Make it your mantra.

At last, you have found your keys under that pile of dirty laundry you couldn't be bothered to do – a laundry bag probably isn't essential since most of your clothes will be strewn across the floor anyway. You've got cash, a camera for plenty of duck-faced selfies and you're ready to hit the dance floor hard. But as dawn breaks and you go to call a taxi you discover that your phone had mutated into a brick. The battery is deader than you feel and all because you left your charger back in Kansas. Well done Dorothy. It may sound trivial, but your phone is a lifeline to the so-called 'real world'. Everyone gets homesick from time to time and being able to call a friend or relative is vital if you hope to retain your sanity. So don't forget that charger.

Fortunately your friend who you met five minutes ago in the local takeaway has ordered a taxi and you're delivered back to university safe and sound, even if, once you reach the bathroom, you're not quite in one piece…

Remember guys, don't forget that toilet brush!

'And Don't Forget Your Toilet Brush'

Sammy Luton

Lancaster University

Sammy's Survival Essentials:

1kg of pasta

An assortment of sauces

Saucepans

Crockery

Alarm clock

Laptop

Two sets of bedding

Photographs of family and friends

'THE POT'

Makeup

Clothes and footwear for all occasions

A winter coat (particularly if your university is in t' North)

Money and a debit card

Passport/ID

Camera

Mobile phone

Mobile/laptop/camera charger

"Pre-drink" alcohol

Paracetamol

Sanitary Towels

Shower gel and Shampoo

Towels

Toothpaste and brush

Toilet paper

Toilet Brush

A University Bucket List

Have an all-nighter and which the sun rise with friends. ☐

Have a BBQ in the snow. ☐

Go to a 'locals' pub with your friends and sit proudly whilst they all try and stare you out. ☐

Visit the local museum/art gallery. ☐

Have a Mexican themed night, full of sombreros, Mexican food and tequila. ☐

Go to the Students Union with you and your friends being the only ones in costumes, a group costume is compulsory. ☐

Have a Disney DVD marathon (for best effects perform this whilst hung-over). ☐

Join a society. ☐

On a night out – salute random strangers to see their reaction. ☐

Cook a meal from every culture. ☐

In the last week of your last year, be able to go into a pub look the bartender straight in the eye and ask for the usual. ☐

Perform a RAG event for charity, skydiving's always one to fall for. ☐

Photobomb. Often. ☐

Have a panicked all-night coursework session the night before a piece of coursework is due in. ☐

Cook a Sunday roast dinner for your flat/ housemates. (See Page 126) ☐

Have a sign put up in a public place banning behaviour because of you. ☐

Go to a music festival. ☐

Go to lots of gigs of never heard of bands in the local area. ☐

Discover a new hobby. ☐

Go on a holiday abroad with your friends, I hear Amsterdam's nice this time of year. ☐

Barter a take away shop to receive food for free or at substantial discount. ☐

Learn a new language. ☐

Live on own brand food for a week. ☐

Go to a lecture still drunk from the night before. ☐

Attend all of your lectures for an entire month. ☐

A Directory of Support

A

University of Aberdeen -
http://www.abdn.ac.uk/student-support/
Aberysthwyth University -
http://www.aber.ac.uk/en/student-support/
Anglia Ruskin University -
http://www.anglia.ac.uk/ruskin/en/home/student_essentials
University of the Arts London -
http://www.arts.ac.uk/study-at-ual/student-support/
Aston University -

http://www1.aston.ac.uk/current-students/health-wellbeing/

B

Bangor University - **http://www.bangor.ac.uk/studentservices/**
University of Bath - **http://www.bath.ac.uk/students/support/**
Bath Spa University -
http://www2.bathspa.ac.uk/services/student-services/
University of Bedfordshire -
https://www.beds.ac.uk/studentlife/student-support
University of Birmingham -
http://www.birmingham.ac.uk/undergraduate/support/
Birmingham City University -
http://www.bcu.ac.uk/student-info/student-services
Bishop Grosseteste University -
http://www.bishopg.ac.uk/?_id=10435

University of Bolton - **http://www.bolton.ac.uk/Students/AdviceAndSupport/**

Bournemouth University - **http://www.bournemouth.ac.uk/academicsupport/**

University of Bradford - **http://www.bradford.ac.uk/student-services/**

University of Brighton -

http://www.brighton.ac.uk/studentlife/

University of Bristol -

http://www.bris.ac.uk/undergraduates/#life

Brunel University - **http://www.brunel.ac.uk/life**

University of Buckingham -

http://www.buckingham.ac.uk/life

C

University of Cambridge -

http://www.cam.ac.uk/current-students/cambridge-life

Canterbury Christ Church -

http://www.canterbury.ac.uk/StudyHere/StudentLife

Cardiff University -

http://www.cardiff.ac.uk/studentsupport/index.html

Cardiff Metropolitan University -

http://www3.cardiffmet.ac.uk/english/studentservices

University of Central Lancashire -

http://www.uclan.ac.uk/study_here/student_support

University of Chester -

http://www.chester.ac.uk/campus-life/support-for-students/

University of Chicester -

http://www.chi.ac.uk/student-life

City University London -

http://www.city.ac.uk/health/support

Coventry University -

http://www.coventry.ac.uk/study-at-coventry/student-support/

Cranfield University -

http://www.cranfield.ac.uk/study/studying-at-cranfield

University of Cumbria -

http://www.cumbria.ac.uk/StudentLife/Support/Home.aspx

D

De Montfort University -

http://www.dmu.ac.uk/study/undergraduate-study/student-support/

University of Derby -

http://www.derby.ac.uk/campus/support/

University of Dundee -

http://www.dundee.ac.uk/studentservices/

Durham University -

https://www.dur.ac.uk/undergraduate/life/

E

University of East Anglia -

http://www.uea.ac.uk/services/students

University of East London -

http://www.uel.ac.uk/students/index.htm

University of Edinburgh -

http://www.ed.ac.uk/staff-students/students/

Edinburgh Napier University -

http://www.napier.ac.uk/study/support/Pages/Support

University of Essex -

http://www.essex.ac.uk/life/

University of Exeter -

http://www.exeter.ac.uk/students/services/

F

Falmouth University - http://www.falmouth.ac.uk/support

G

University of Glasgow - http://www.gla.ac.uk/studentlife/support/

Glasgow Caledonian University -

http://www.gcu.ac.uk/student/index.html

University of Gloucestershire -

http://www.glos.ac.uk/supporting/Pages/default.aspx

University of Greenwich -

http://www2.gre.ac.uk/study/support

Glyndwr University -

http://www.glyndwr.ac.uk/en/Studentsupport/

H

Harper Adams University - **http://www.harper-adams.ac.uk/student-services/**

Heriot-Watt University - **http://www.hw.ac.uk/students/student-services.htm**

University of Hertfordshire - **http://www.herts.ac.uk/university-life/student-support**

University of the Highlands and Islands - **http://www.uhi.ac.uk/en/students/support**

University of Huddersfield - **http://www.hud.ac.uk/students/**

University of Hull -

http://www2.hull.ac.uk/student/support.aspx

I

Imperial College London -

http://www3.imperial.ac.uk/students

K

Keele University - **http://www.keele.ac.uk/ssds/**

University of Kent - **http://www.kent.ac.uk/student/index.html**

Kingston University - **http://www.kingston.ac.uk/**

L

Lancaster University - **http://www.lancaster.ac.uk/sbs/**

University of Leeds -

http://www.llc.leeds.ac.uk/students/student-support

Leeds Metropolitan University -
https://www.leedsmet.ac.uk/life/index.htm
Leeds Trinity University -
http://www.leedstrinity.ac.uk/services/pages/default.aspx
University of Leicester - **http://www2.le.ac.uk/students**
University of Lincoln -
http://www.lincoln.ac.uk/home/campuslife/
University of Liverpool - **http://www.liv.ac.uk/my-liverpool/**
Liverpool Hope University -
http://www.hope.ac.uk/lifeathope/
Liverpool John Moores University -
http://ljmu.ac.uk/Life-at-LJMU/
University of London -
http://www.london.ac.uk/student_services.html
Royal Holloway University of London -
http://www.rhul.ac.uk/studentlife/home.aspx
University College London - **http://www.ucl.ac.uk/students/**
London Metropolitan University -
http://www.londonmet.ac.uk/services/
London South Bank University -
http://www.lsbu.ac.uk/student-life/student-services
Loughborough University -

http://www.lboro.ac.uk/students/

M

University of Manchester -
http://www.manchester.ac.uk/undergraduate/studentlife/
Manchester Metropolitan University -
http://www.mmu.ac.uk/sas/studentservices/

Middlesex University -

http://www.mdx.ac.uk/facilities/support/

N

Newcastle University -
http://www.ncl.ac.uk/students/wellbeing
Newman University -
http://www.newman.ac.uk/student-support/
University of Northampton -
http://www.northampton.ac.uk/students/student-support
Northumbria University -
http://www.northumbria.ac.uk/sd/student/
Norwich University of the Arts -
http://www.nua.ac.uk/study/support/
University of Nottingham -
http://www.nottingham.ac.uk/currentstudents/index.aspx
Nottingham Trent University -
http://www.ntu.ac.uk/student_services/index.html

O

University of Oxford - **http://www.ox.ac.uk/students/living/**

P

University of Plymouth -
http://www1.plymouth.ac.uk/studentgateway/
University of Portsmouth -

http://www.port.ac.uk/students/

Q

Queen's University Belfast -
http://www.qub.ac.uk/home/TheUniversity/GeneralServices/

Queen Margaret University -

**http://www.qmu.ac.uk/prospective_students/student_
services/**

R

University of Reading - **http://www.reading.ac.uk/life/**
The Robert Gordon University -
http://www.rgu.ac.uk/student-life
Roehampton University -
http://www.roehampton.ac.uk/Services/
Royal Agricultural University -

http://www.rau.ac.uk/student-life

S

University of St. Andrews -
http://www.st-andrews.ac.uk/students/advice/
University of St. Mark & St. John -
http://www.marjon.ac.uk/student-life/
University of Sheffield -
http://www.sheffield.ac.uk/undergraduate/why
Sheffield Hallam University -
http://www.shu.ac.uk/currentstudents/support/
University of Southampton -
http://www.southampton.ac.uk/undergraduate/studentlife
Southampton Solent University -

143

http://www.solent.ac.uk/student-life/

University of South Wales - **http://www.southwales.ac.uk/student/life**

Staffordshire University -

http://www.staffs.ac.uk/study/services/

University of Stirling -

http://www.stir.ac.uk/campus-life/

University of Strathclyde -

http://www.strath.ac.uk/campuslife/

University of Sunderland -

 http://www.sunderland.ac.uk/studentlife/

University of Surrey -

http://www.surrey.ac.uk/currentstudents/

University of Sussex -

http://www.sussex.ac.uk/students/support/

Swansea University -

http://www.swansea.ac.uk/dace/students/studentsupport/

T

Teeside University - **http://www.tees.ac.uk/sections/stud/**

U

University of Ulster - http://www.ulster.ac.uk/life/

W

University of Warwick -

http://www2.warwick.ac.uk/services/student-support-services

University of West London -

 http://www.uwl.ac.uk/students/support-services-for-students

University of Westminster -

http://www.westminster.ac.uk/study/prospective-students

University of West of England - **http://www1.uwe.ac.uk/students/studysupport**

University of West of Scotland -

http://www.uws.ac.uk/current-students/

University of Winchester -

http://www.winchester.ac.uk/startinghere/

University of Wolverhampton -

http://www.wlv.ac.uk/default.aspx?page=9182

University of Worcester -

http://www.worcester.ac.uk/your-home.html

Y

University of York - **https://www.york.ac.uk/students/**

York St John University -

http://www.yorksj.ac.uk/students.aspx

fterwords, n.

LAMPLIGHT
◀ press ▶

Lamplight Press was established in 2013. We are one of the few publishing companies in the world who are entirely ran by university students. We are situated at Loughborough University, catering to the academic and creative community around the UK.

Working with *The Student Wordsmith* has been an absolute pleasure and we're all very pleased with the outcome of our year's work. Hopefully the relationship between Lamplight Press and *The Student Wordsmith* will continue to be strong over the coming years and there can be many more projects in the future.

A special thanks to the company's founding members and managers in its first year of life to:

Dr Melanie Ramdarshan Bold – Director and Founder

Dr Kerry Featherstone – Chair of the Editorial Board

Becky Wheeler – Marketing and Legal Manager

Maria Convey – Editorial Manager

Sian Caton & **Aaron Price** – Social Media Managers

Becky Denton – Communications Manager

Joey Amoah – Digital and Finance Manager

Josh Moses – Design and Marketing Manager

David Keown – Webmaster and Production Manager

Launched on 17 April 2013, The Student Wordsmith is an award-winning, online writing and publishing platform aimed, predominantly, at a creative student and graduate audience.

Having commercialised its first book this year in the collaborative collection, You is for University, the not-for-profit organisation is passionate about showcasing emerging young talent in this way.

Endeavouring to expand into other creative industries by publishing for them, building portfolios and encouraging a budding creative community, The Student Wordsmith is 'here to inspire creativity […] that focuses on the useful, meaningful, and important topics of everyday life.'

The Student Wordsmith was named the Overall Winner of Loughborough University's Graduate Enterprise Award at this year's ceremony in April.

For more information on the products and services The Student Wordsmith offers, visit www.thestudentwordsmith.com.